THE TRIUMPH TR
From 20TS to TR6

John Nikas

Photography by Marc Vorgers

AMBERLEY

First published 2018

Amberley Publishing
The Hill, Stroud
Gloucestershire, GL5 4EP

www.amberley-books.com

Copyright © John Nikas, 2018
Photographs copyright © Marc Vorgers

The right of John Nikas to be identified as the
Author of this work has been asserted in
accordance with the Copyright, Designs and
Patents Act 1988.

ISBN 978 1 4456 7382 0 (print)
ISBN 978 1 4456 7383 7 (ebook)

British Library Cataloguing in Publication Data.
A catalogue record for this book is available from
the British Library.

Typeset in 10pt on 13pt Celeste.
Origination by Amberley Publishing.
Printed in the UK.

Contents

Chapter 1
From Bicycles to Motorcars

Triumph's roots sprung from a small firm established by Siegfried Bettman to import sewing machines from Germany and the United States. Born in Nuremberg to merchant parents in 1863, Bettman departed for London soon after his twenty-first birthday and found employment as a clerk and translator for a small publishing house. Working in an office, however, grew tiresome after only six months and he left for a position with the White Sewing Machine Company as a Foreign Correspondent.

Despite limited experience in either sales or customer relations, Bettman was an enthusiastic beginner, travelling as far afield as North Africa to peddle his wares. From a new home base in Coventry, he sourced equipment from other manufacturers to broaden his catalogue and began to search for additional products that could be sold to his existing customers.

Bettman did not have to look far for an idea. As bicycles rose to become the most popular form of personal transportation in the late nineteenth century, a number of manufacturers, most of them concentrated in the West Midlands, began to build them alongside the watches, clocks, bullets and machine tools that they already built. With so many potential vendors located in such close proximity, Bettman saw the potential in the growing transportation market and decided to offer bicycles for sale alongside his other goods.

Within a few months, the demand for bicycles threatened to overwhelm the small enterprise. Eager to take advantage of the situation, Bettman reached an agreement with a firm in Birmingham to build a bicycle that could be sold more profitably than those he was currently offering for sale. Looking for a name that would have broad international appeal and could be understood in various languages, Bettman chose the 'Triumph' trade name, which soon became the most popular brand his firm sold.

Triumph's potential was not lost on others. The Dunlop Pneumatic Tire Company provided Bettman with financing in 1887, which provided the company with the resources to procure additional product. Later that year Bettman partnered with Mauritz Johann Schulte, a fellow German émigré whose strategic vision would prove crucial in the coming years. The pair soon agreed that they should manufacture their own bicycles to reduce manufacturing costs and increase profits.

In short order, a suitable factory was located in Coventry and the first bicycles that the company manufactured were sold in 1889. Even with Dunlop's previous investment, Triumph suffered from severe undercapitalisation, which would become a hallmark of the brand throughout its existence. Burdened by a lack of cash to pay the monthly bills and finance future growth, Bettman and Schulte were forced to solicit funds from investors on a regular basis. Despite the limited

Siegfried Bettman, seen in his ceremonial robe that he wore as the Mayor of Coventry from 1913 to 1914, the first non-British subject to hold the office. Although his Germanic roots forced his removal at the start of the First World War, his contributions to his adopted homeland cannot be disputed. In addition to his important contributions to Triumph and Standard, he also created a charitable foundation that helped individuals start their own businesses. (British Sports Car Hall of Fame)

operating capital and burdensome debt, the bicycle line found more customers and soon attracted greater attention throughout the industry.

As sales increased, Triumph focused on further growth, creating a German subsidiary in 1896 that was known as Orial Triumph Werke Nürnberg AG. Not long afterwards, however, consumer demand fell as interest in motorised cycles increased. This development was no surprise, especially to Schulte, who had long argued that the company should install an engine on a reinforced cycle frame to create a proper motorbike. The proposal made obvious sense, since it naturally complemented the bicycle line and reduced the risk that a downturn in either market could threaten the whole operation.

Trusty by Name, Trusty by Nature

Although there was significant internal support for Schulte's plan, it took some time to implement, delaying the first Triumph motorcycle until 1902. In those early days, building an engine was beyond the means of most small manufacturers, forcing Triumph to use a Belgian Minerva that made 2¼ horsepower for that first model. Over the next three years, the company continued to use powerplants bought from larger manufacturers, but a proprietary design that would change Triumph's fortunes forever appeared in 1905. The new engine allowed the bike to cruise at 30 mph and the simple construction kept the purchase price at an affordable level. With sales increasing each year, the company abandoned the

5

works on Much Park Street and moved into new quarters on Priory Street in 1907. Only two years later, sales reached almost 9,000 units, but even better results were on the horizon.

As Triumph motorcycles continued their successful run, Reginald Maudslay was establishing the Standard Motor Company across town to build automobiles, which he thought would soon replace the motorcycle as the dominant form of personal transport.

The new company was founded on the premise that all its models would use interchangeable parts to reduce costs and simplify maintenance, making the moniker an important marketing element. Rapid growth and heavy competition caused this charter to be dropped, but the cars continued to be manufactured as Standards. Almost from the start, the company developed an enviable reputation for engineering excellence, building one of the few six-cylinder engines offered in a British car (along with Rolls-Royce and Napier) and maintaining admirable quality throughout the line.

Nonetheless, Standard found it difficult to turn a profit. By 1912, Maudslay needed cash to buy out a troublesome partner and meet the daily expenses. Bettman was among those that offered to help, but the assistance came at the price of installing him as the firm's chairman. With no other alternative, Maudslay agreed to the terms, allowing Bettman to helm both Standard and Triumph, although he would give up the former position upon the start of the First World War.

Trusty Triumphs served across every front during the First World War, earning a reputation as the best motorcycles used in the conflict. This image shows Corporal Oswald H. Davis (far right) astride the Model H that he used to carry pigeons and deliver messages on the Western Front. (Philip Holdway-Davis)

As the British Expeditionary Force prepared to sail across the Channel to France in 1914, the War Office placed an order for 100 Model H motorcycles for immediate delivery. Although not far removed from the standard civilian models, their durability and performance soon endeared them to the British and allied servicemen that rode them across the conflict's various operating theatres. More than 30,000 examples had been delivered for military use by the end of hostilities, cementing the company's reputation in the process. Known as 'Trusty Triumphs', they were among the most popular and effective motorbikes of the war, which helped account for their success with civilian customers as soon as peace returned.

Within the first year after the Armistice, Triumph was the best-selling motorcycle brand in England, which provided the company with the money needed to commence automobile production.

For the Greater Glory

In the post-war marketplace, most of the country's motorcycle manufacturers had already added automobiles to their existing range, but Triumph was hesitant to join them. As was the case when the company shifted from bicycle to motorbike production, Schulte was the driving force behind the transition. As early as 1903, he had experimented with a motorised tricycle, but the plans were put on hold to allow the factory to focus more attention on the profitable motorcycle line. Over the next fifteen years, Schulte continued to agitate for the automobile, but Bettman refused to shift significant resources away from the popular Model H.

In 1919, the debate finally reached a boil, even as engineers were hard at work on a prototype saloon. Frustrated at the slow pace of progress, Schulte parted company with his old partner, leaving the company bereft of his vision and drive. Two years later, Triumph had the opportunity to acquire the assets of the struggling Morris operation, but Bettman refused, choosing instead to acquire the manufacturing facilities that had once belonged to the Dawson Car Company.

With all these machinations behind the scenes, Triumph's first automobile, designated the 10/20, did not reach customers until 1923. Additional models soon followed, however, each successively larger and more sophisticated, featuring innovations such as hydraulic brakes and four-wheel dampers. The automotive press received them enthusiastically, praising in particular their refinement and impressive styling. Most customers, however, did not want or could not afford such large cars, forcing Triumph to build something smaller to appeal to the common man.

Although MG would soon dominate the marketplace for small, affordable sporting cars, Triumph entered the arena first with the diminutive Super Seven in 1927. Rugged and reasonably fast, it was an instant success on the rally and trials circuit. Among the ranks of the drivers that won with the little car was Donald Healey, who drove his Triumph to seventh overall in the Monte Carlo Rally and an overall victory at Brighton.

Produced in response to the successful Austin 7, Triumph produced the Super 7 from 1927 to 1934. Although the top speed of the standard models was less than 50 mph, they proved reliable and robust in competition. In addition to Donald Healey's exploits, Victor Horsman had great success in 1929 and 1930 with his specials, while the little car shone in endurance events in America and Australia around the same time. (Graham Robson Collection).

Buoyed by the Super Seven's competition success and the publicity it generated, Triumph started to expand the range, offering ten distinct models from family saloons to small coupés by 1930. Although interest in the smaller cars continued through the first years of the Depression, sales of the larger models began to flag. Rather than stand pat, Triumph chose to push upmarket, introducing the Super Eight, Super Nine and Scorpion in 1932.

With nicer appointments and better performance, the new models were more expensive and complex, forcing the company into more competitive waters. In order to increase sales, Triumph started to export cars throughout the British Commonwealth, where features such as right-hand steering, narrow bodies and lower top speeds were acceptable traits. Among the most important of these markets were Australia and New Zealand, which was recognised when the Southern Cross was introduced in 1932.

Bettman retired, rather reluctantly, the following year, missing out on the introduction of the Glorias, which became known as the 'Smartest Cars in the Land'. The first variant was introduced in late 1933 and the range eventually encompassed saloons, touring cars and sports cars, many of which are considered among the finest examples from the pre-war era.

As the Gloria neared production, Triumph lured Donald Healey away from Riley to supervise product development and manage the competition programme. The hiring soon paid dividends as Healey helped develop the Monte Carlo Tourer, even driving an example to a class win and third overall in the 1934 Monte Carlo Rally. The unexpected finish garnered significant attention, with one publication noting that, 'Triumph has leapt into the front rank of famous marques.'

Donald Healey (behind the wheel) and Jack Ridley with a Gloria Speed Model Tourer. The pair were Triumph's most successful drivers in the pre-war era, each winning honours in the Monte Carlo Rally. (Graham Robson Collection)

Donald Healey behind the wheel of a 1936 Gloria Six. Built at a new factory on the Foleshill Hill side of Coventry, the Glorias were among the last successful models that Triumph had before it entered receivership only three years later. (Graham Robson Collection)

Encouraged by the positive showing at Monte Carlo, Triumph management wanted to field an entry in the 2-litre class, which heretofore had been the exclusive domain of the world's most famous marques. With a recent promotion to the role of technical director, Healey set out to design a vehicle that could compete with the best in class. Faced with such a daunting task, Healey followed the advice of motoring journalist Tommy Wisdom, who suggested that it would be faster to construct a tool room replica of the Alfa Romeo 8C 2300, rather than starting out from a blank page.

With a single example of the world-class sports car procured, Healey had his technicians disassemble the vehicle and then carefully reverse engineered the individual components. Once the work was well underway, Healey journeyed to Milan to secure blessing for his project from Vittorio Jano, Alfa Romeo's legendary chief engineer. Using considerable charm and his skills at persuasion, Healey secured the permission that he sought, allowing the project to venture forth from the shadows into the light.

Despite many similarities, Healey's Dolomite Straight 8 differed in detail from its Italian inspiration, incorporating a smaller 1,991cc engine, an Armstrong-Siddeley pre-selector gearbox, Hartford friction dampers, stronger leaf springs, Lockheed hydraulic drum brakes and a more robust chassis to survive the gruelling rallies that the car was built to win. Notwithstanding

9

Donald Healey and the Dolomite Straight Eight near his family home in Perranporth, Cornwall. Bearing the registration ADU 4, Healey drove this example in the 1935 Monte Carlo Rally, where it was destroyed in a collision with a train. (British Sports Car Hall of Fame)

the purloined design, it was hailed as a technological marvel, receiving almost universal praise from the motoring press that first saw it at the 1934 London Motor Show.

The Dolomite's competition debut was rather mixed as Triumph's lead car collided with a train at an unguarded railroad crossing during the 1935 Monte Carlo Rally. Driving through a dense fog on the Jutland peninsula, Donald Healey slowed abruptly, fearing that the supercharger was about to seize. Instead, the apparent whistling was an oncoming train that destroyed the car and almost killed both driver and navigator. Jack Ridley placed second overall and won class laurels in his Gloria Special, helping to make up for the near calamity with the Dolomite. The Dolomite returned to Monte Carlo the following year, finishing at eighth overall with the best showing for a British team, but management soon decided to abandon the expensive project in favour of models that could generate actual profits.

During the previous year, Triumph had taken a huge gamble and purchased a new dedicated automotive production facility, but the move came at an inopportune time as sales fell even further, reducing the amount of available money. Even with fewer distinct variants to build in 1936 – several Gloria models having been discontinued – profits were thin, forcing the sale of the motorcycle business to raise operating capital. Without the motorcycle profits to subsidize the automotive business, sales fell to fewer than 1,000 units, worsening the financial picture considerably.

With a worsening financial position, Triumph reluctantly decided to sell the motorcycle business and use the proceeds to purchase a new factory for production of the Gloria range. Among the most expensive models was this 1935 Gloria Vitesse Six Tourer that carried a £385 purchase price. Built on a 116-inch wheelbase and powered by a 1,991cc six-cylinder engine, only five examples are known to have survived into the present day.

Walter Belgrove designed this lovely mascot for the radiator cap to imbue the Glorias with an aura of speed and luxury.

The introduction of a new model range, called the Dolomite to honour the Alfa-based competition car, helped boost sales temporarily, but demand soon fell back to earth. With no other alternative than to seek outside assistance, Donald Healey was made a director and charged with finding a suitable merger partner. Discussions with Riley failed, after it chose a better offer from Lord Nuffield, and then, following several abortive efforts to raise cash from other sources, Triumph entered receivership during the summer of 1939.

The company's assets were sold to Thos. W. Ward Ltd., which was formally announced on 1 September 1939, not long after German tanks began to roll across the Polish frontier. The sudden onset of hostilities surprised the new owners, who had intended to sell Triumph's assets piecemeal to maximise the potential profits, but the oncoming conflict put those plans on hold.

In order to buy some time until a buyer could be found for the Coventry factories, which were the most valuable assets, Healey was asked to remain as General Manager to oversee the company's transition into the production of armaments for the war effort. Under his watch, the few workers that remained on staff focused on aircraft carburettor work and the excess space on the floor was rented out to manufacture fuselages for the Armstrong-Whitworth Albemarle.

With so much of England's industrial capacity concentrated in Coventry and elsewhere in the West Midlands, the region became a priority for the Luftwaffe. There were several smaller attacks made during the Battle of Britain, but the massive bombing raid that took place during the night of 14 November 1940 caused unprecedented destruction for a civilian target. More than 500 bombers struck in the darkness, damaging most of the factories in the city and destroying more than 4,300 homes.

Triumph's original motorcycle factory, which had been under separate ownership since 1936, was demolished, while the automotive production facilities were heavily damaged. With so much destruction to the company's principal asset, the new owners postponed plans to sell off the remaining assets. German bombers would return again over the next two years, causing even more damage, but one of the greatest losses came when Healey left for the Rootes Group, where he worked on armoured car development.

Despite his departure, Healey remained in close contact with his former colleagues at Triumph, allowing him to plan for an eventual return after the war to build a new sports car that he was developing in his spare time. By 1944, Healey was ready to present his plans to the management at Wards, who initially seemed receptive to the proposal. After some consideration, however, the proposal was rejected on the grounds that Healey lacked the proper manufacturing experience, which seemed curious considering that he had already served the company in several executive capacities.

Having rejected Healey, Wards set out to find a buyer for the damaged factories and the Triumph name, which were the only assets with value that remained. Of the potential candidates, Ford and Vauxhall were dismissed out of hand, while Austin and Nuffield were considered too large to bother with the shambles that the marque had become. The remaining possibilities were the Standard Motor Company that Bettman had helped to save before the First World War, and the Rootes Group, which already owned Hillman, Humber, Sunbeam and Talbot.

In the three decades since Bettman's involvement, Standard had prospered, building sensible family automobiles and providing components for smaller manufacturers such as Morgan and Swallow to use in their own products. Much of the success that the company had achieved could be credited to Sir John Black, who had become a managing director in 1933. Under his leadership, Standard was an early proponent of the wartime shadow factory programme and had begun to plan for a return to civilian production well before hostilities ended.

Despite his mercurial personality and troublesome reputation, Black was a visionary who believed that Triumph's pre-war reputation for performance and

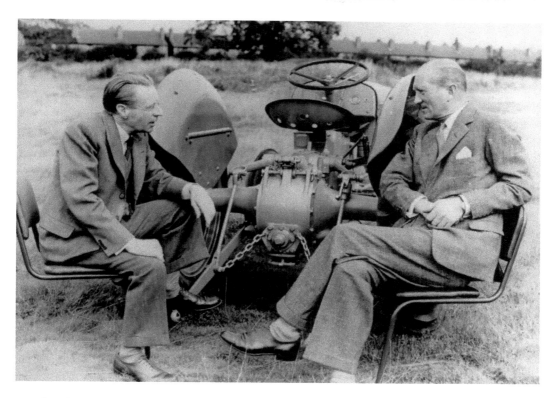

Sir John Black and Harry Ferguson sitting beside the tractor that Standard would start manufacturing in 1946, helping to make possible the growth that would eventually spawn the TR sports car series. It would receive the Vanguard engine in 1947. (Graham Robson Collection)

engineering excellence could act as the linchpin to a burgeoning automotive empire. Better yet, Triumph's experience with sports cars might also help Black compete with Sir William Lyons, who had used various Standard components to create several successful sporting models at SS-Jaguar before the war.

Standard purchased Triumph on 24 November 1944, and held its first board meeting less than a month before the war ended in Europe. Not long afterwards, Black also reached an agreement with Harry Ferguson to manufacture light tractors at the former shadow factory at Banner Lane. More importantly, he had convinced the tractor magnate to allow the use of a new engine that was then under development at Standard, which would have a significant impact on Triumph's future sports cars.

The first post-war model that Standard introduced was the Vanguard, powered by a modified version of the engine used in the Ferguson tractor. With contemporary styling and good performance, it was an immediate hit with customers around the world, especially in traditional export markets such as Australia and New Zealand. But notwithstanding the Vanguard's success, Black wanted something even more spectacular for his various holdings, particularly in regards to Triumph. It would take a while for him to get his wish.

13

Chapter 2
A New Sports Car Standard

Black determined that Triumph would start with two models, a saloon and a touring roadster. Both would benefit from experience gained building aircraft during the war, relying on tube frames and aluminium bodywork, but with little money available it would be imperative to incorporate as many existing Standard components as possible.

It was no secret that Black wanted a proper sports car, so much so that he personally supervised development of the touring roadster in the hope that it could become such an automobile, rather like Jaguar's SS100 from right before the war. Despite an aluminium body, the vehicle was rather heavy and curiously styled, blending an amalgam of pre-war design cues with bulbous front wings and a rounded tail that housed a dickey seat, a blaring anachronism for the time. Because supplies of the Vanguard engine were limited, the new model made do with the same 1,776cc, four-cylinder unit that Jaguar had used for the last of its pre-war models. Introduced in March 1946, Triumph's 1800 Roadster failed to gain much traction in the market, even after it became the 2000 Roadster

Ken Rawlings built his *Buttercup* special in 1950 using a number of Standard components including a Flying Eight chassis and Vanguard engine and gearbox. Although Harry Webster and others deny that it influenced the development of the Triumph sports car project, it certainly showed the potential that existed in the humble assemblage of parts. (Graham Robson Collection)

Intended to replace the 1800 Roadster, Walter Belgrove's TRX was too complex and expensive for series production. Built on a thinly modified Standard Vanguard chassis, the TRX used the Vanguard's 2,088cc engine fitted with an experimental crossflow cylinder head and dual SU carburettors that increased output to 71 bhp. The distinctive bodywork was fashioned by Helliwells. (Graham Robson Collection)

in 1949, marking the installation of the Vanguard's 2,088cc powerplant. It was discontinued after only a year on the market.

Black refused to abandon his sports car dreams, asking Walter Belgrove, Triumph's design chief, to fashion a more appropriate and compelling shape for a sports car than the 1800 and 2000 Roadsters had worn. Having been unavailable when those models were designed, Belgrove approached his task with an eye towards something far more modern. What resulted appeared for the first time at the 1950 Paris Auto Salon, wearing futuristic envelope coachwork fashioned from double-wall aluminium. Named the TRX, it was overly complex, featuring electro-hydraulically operated headlamps, seats and bonnet, which would have made it prohibitively expensive to produce in mass quantities. Since Standard could not find time to fashion the requisite bodywork tooling, Belgrove approached several Italian coachbuilders to handle the job, but these options also failed and the project was then abandoned.

The failure to produce a proper sporting Triumph was weighing heavily against Black, especially in consideration of the profits that Jaguar and MG were

The 1947 Triumph 1800 Roadster was the company's first attempt to develop a sporting model that Sir John Black hoped could compete with Jaguar. Displaying styling from Frank Callaby that blended modern themes with some anachronistic touches, the final product looked too bloated for its intended purpose.

There is no question that this is the most elegant instrument panel to feature in a post-war Triumph convertible. Among the luxurious interior appointments were polished wood door caps, wool carpets, and attractive instruments that were centrally located to support both left and right-hand drive applications.

The 1800 Roadster featured the same overhead valve 1,776cc powerplant and transmission that had been supplied to SS-Jaguar, though a column-shifter was fitted for this application. The 2000 Roadster would use the 2,088cc Vanguard engine during its brief production run.

The most unique feature of the Triumph Roadsters was the dickey seat, which by this time was a decidedly dated feature. The passengers in the back were protected from the wind with a collapsible screen, but they had to access the compartment by stepping on the extreme edge of the rear bumper.

reaping from the lucrative North American export market. Faced with the reality that the former was too sophisticated to challenge with the available resources, he set his sights on the more affordable end of the spectrum, where MG was finding so much success.

The Inspiration Game

Around the same time, Black was shown the potential that existed when the Vanguard engine was paired with a competent chassis – as the Morgan Plus 4 would also prove – in the form of the *Buttercup* special constructed by Ken Rawlings. An employee of the Standard-Triumph distributor in Birmingham, he had mated the Vanguard engine with a modified Standard Eight chassis to create a competent sports car. Undeniably rough around the edges, *Buttercup* foreshadowed many of the traits that would mark the later TR series: rugged construction, functional styling and superior performance. Best of all, it had not cost much to build and was finished in less than six months, despite work taking place only at night and on weekends.

Whether Black was personally aware of the *Buttercup* project during its construction is subject to debate, but there is no question that the crude little sports car came to the attention of Triumph management soon after completion. It did not take long for them to wonder what Triumph could achieve in a similar fashion with access to better resources and facilities.

Because MG was increasing market share with each day that passed, Triumph's most pressing issue was time. Perhaps unwilling to devote further resources to the challenge of developing another new model from scratch, Black approached Morgan with an offer to purchase the small family-owned firm. The overture made obvious sense since Morgan had just ordered the Vanguard engine for the new Plus 4 and had used the Flying Ten engine in the pre-war 4/4, providing much familiarity between the parties. After several weeks of contemplation, however, Morgan declined the proposal, trusting Black's word that the negative response would not hinder the future supply of Standard engines.

At this point, Black wanted to reach the market in the most expedient manner possible and instructed Belgrove to take another crack at a new design, hinting that the MG TD could be used as inspiration for his effort. Belgrove took umbrage at the suggestion and dismissed it out of hand. He had instead preferred to explore some of the concepts that appeared in the TRX, but he was allocated just £16,000 for tooling and instructed to finish the job in as little time as possible, rendering that prospect impracticable. With Belgrove working on a fresh exterior shape, Harry Webster and John Turnbull set about developing an appropriate chassis to mate with the Vanguard engine that would power the new sports car.

Dubbed the 20TS, the effort was a passable result given the limited time and money allocated to the project. Unlike the advanced TRX, Belgrove came up with a shape that was almost wholly devoid of compound curves and hard to manufacture panels. The bobbed tail housed an exposed spare tire, made necessary by the modified frame used, that was out of harmony with the rest of the car, but the design forward of the rear axle would make the eventual transition to the TR2.

Unhappy with the suggestion that he should ape the design of the rival MG TD, Walter Belgrove designed a modern shape for the 20TS. With a tooling budget of £16,000, every step was taken to eliminate styling elements that would have been costly to reproduce. (Graham Robson Collection)

The 20TS bodyshell undergoing work in the factory. The prototype was constructed in under three months, with Ted Grinham and his staff working long hours to ready the car for its introduction at Earls Court in October 1952. (Graham Robson Collection)

20TS in the workshop displaying signs from recent road usage. The original frame was cobbled together from a spare Standard Flying Eight chassis, but it was significantly altered to achieve the 88-inch wheelbase and correct mounting points for the Mayflower-based independent front suspension and rear axle assembly. (Graham Robson Collection)

20TS at the 1952 London Motor Show at Earls Court. With an estimated £555 purchase price, it would have slotted in between the MG TD and Morgan Plus 4. Unfortunately, Donald Healey introduced his Hundred at the same event, causing a stir in the motoring press and forcing Triumph to implement changes that would make 20TS more competitive. (Graham Robson Collection)

Underneath the skin was a ladder frame with an 88-inch wheelbase that had been cobbled together from existing stores of Flying Nine parts, while the independent front suspension came from the Mayflower saloon. To allow competition in the 2-litre class, new wet cylinder liners and pistons were fitted to the Vanguard's 2,088cc engine to reduce the displacement to 1,991cc. In this form, the engine produced 75 bhp at 4,300 rpm, which was thought sufficient to attain the performance desired.

Having rushed to create the prototype, Triumph was determined to display the 20TS at the 1952 London Motor Show, which would also mark the debut of the Healey Hundred. While reaction to the 20TS from the press and public was rather restrained, the Hundred was lavished with praise for its handsome shape and top speed performance in excess of 100 mph. Before the show was over, Healey had reached an agreement with Sir Leonard Lord that BMC would produce the roadster in volume as soon as possible, sucking all the wind from out of Triumph's sails.

Faced with the Hundred's unexpected appearance, Triumph's design and engineering staff worked to rectify the myriad problems that besotted the 20TS, hoping to have a redesigned model finished by the following spring so it could compete with the newly minted Austin-Healey 100. Their primary concern dealt with performance, since it was apparent that the new challenger would have no trouble besting what could be expected from the 20TS.

To see what the car was actually like to drive on the road, Triumph sought the assistance of Ken Richardson, who had worked on BRM's Grand Prix efforts and had a sound reputation as a capable test driver. Shortly after the close of the show, he was provided the opportunity to drive the car around the Coventry factory, which resulted in his oft-reported conclusion that, 'It's a bloody death trap!' Although unflattering to the hastily constructed prototype, it was precisely the unvarnished truth that needed to be uttered if the 20TS could become the sports car that Black and Triumph wanted.

Disappointed with his expert evaluation, Black asked what improvements were needed to set the car right. Richardson responded that the 20TS needed more power and a stronger chassis if it were to have any chance at success. In addition, Triumph also wanted to address criticism of the exterior styling, leaving little time to implement such important changes.

Typically for Triumph, money and time were short, so rather than construct a new prototype, parts from the finished 20TS show car and a second partially completed vehicle were used to develop their successors. The frame was substantially redesigned for greater stiffness and strength, while the brakes were improved for better stopping power. Outside, the entire design of the car from behind the doors was abandoned to incorporate a longer tail with an opening boot lid, addressing concerns about the ungainly appearance and lack of storage space.

The most important work, however, was lavished on the engine, which would need more power and better reliability to compete against the Austin-Healey and a recently announced new model from Abingdon called the MG TF. Even more surprising news came from across town, when Sunbeam revealed that a specially modified version of the new Alpine had reached 120 mph at the Jabbeke Highway in Belgium. With such worthy competitors, Triumph doubled down on its efforts to improve performance, circling the test track at the Motor Industry Research Association for hours, waiting for something to break so that the component could be redesigned and strengthened.

On 20 May 1953, Triumph was ready to see what it had accomplished over the past five months, sending the second prototype across to Belgium for a record attempt at Jabbeke. Built with several parts and the forward half of the body from the partially completed second 20TS prototype, it bore the registration number MVC 575. It boasted a host of aerodynamic modifications, including a racing windscreen, metal tonneau cover, undertray and rear wheel spats that Triumph hoped could better help it slice through the air.

Fresh from its record-breaking run at the Jabbeke highway on 20 May 1953, MVC 575 is featured on display at the Belgian Auto Salon. In speed trim it would cover the flying kilometre at 124.889, and 114.890 mph over the same distance in touring trim with overdrive. This historic vehicle has been fully restored to original condition and remains in the United Kingdom, where it has appeared at a number of major classic car events. (Karl Ludvigsen)

A 1954 TR2 long door example finished in a striking livery of black over red. The zipper on the sidescreen allowed the owner to reach inside and operate a pull cord to open the door. Note the lack of trim around the grille opening and the starting handle mount forward of the mesh grille.

A 1955 TR2 short door variant. The hood material and sidescreen design on this example do not appear original, although the level of fit and finish is impressive. The outer sill is now visible below the lower edge of the short door.

The long door variant of the TR2 existed until October 1954 at Commission Number TS4002. The change was made because the long door panel could not be opened when the low car was parked too close to a high kerb. Note that the corner of the door card has a sharp corner in contrast to the rounded corner seen on the late TR3A.

This 1954 TR2 is a short door example finished in olive yellow over blackberry. Around 100 examples were finished in this striking hue from 1953 to 1954 according to marque historian Bill Piggott. Note the remote switch for the Laycock de Normanville overdrive on the extreme left of the dash panel.

The TR2 made good use of the 1,991cc four-cylinder engine sourced from the Standard Vanguard. The powerplant produced 90 bhp at 4,800 rpm on an 8.5:1 compression ratio that was selected to compensate for the variable petrol quality that was still prevalent at the time. Despite the 92 mm stroke it was an efficient unit that returned 34.68 mpg during the 1954 24 Hours of Le Mans. The valve cover is correctly painted in black, but the finish on this example should be smoother.

The TR2 featured a spacious and well-appointed interior that was finished in attractive materials that were comparable in quality to those used on the more expensive Austin-Healey 100. The plug behind the shift lever is to allow access to the grease nipple on the propeller shaft.

The external hinges and wing beading were painted body colour throughout the TR2's production run, except for some very late examples that had chrome bonnet hinges. The windscreen is secured with two Dzus quick-release fasteners to facilitate removal for competition use. This interesting feature remained in place until the late TR3A appeared.

This early example is fitted with the Lucas 471 tail lamp that was in use through Commission Number TS1306 and the additional reflector that became mandatory in the United Kingdom in 1953/54. The centrally mounted Lucas 525 assembly illuminated in both red and white to serve as a rear and number plate lamp.

With Richardson behind the wheel, the first run was a disappointment at just over 104 mph. The dismal result was due to a loose spark plug wire, which was soon remedied, allowing the car to set out again on another two-way test run. This time MVC 575 performed flawlessly, recording an impressive average speed of 124.8 mph. Better yet, in standard touring trim it still made 114 mph, which would lead the way at the affordable end of the market and had even exceeded the performance of Healey's Hundred at the same venue. At last, Sir John Black had a sports car that he would be proud to call a Triumph.

Ready and Willing

The newly christened TR2 officially debuted at the 1953 Geneva Auto Salon, winning plaudits from the assembled masses. Although objective observers would concede that it lacked the same beauty as the Austin-Healey, Triumph's new sports car was about as fast, despite an engine that was almost 700cc smaller, and more affordable, becoming the cheapest sports car in the world that could surpass 100 mph. The new box section chassis was incredibly stout, and the solid foundation bestowed a similar character to the rest of the car.

Although the ride was firm and the overall presentation was noisy and crude, it was fast and rugged, leading one journalist to write 'the new Triumph is a hairy-chested, flame-spitting wildcat', while another said the acceleration seemed jet-assisted. Tooling delays meant that few examples were built in 1953, failing to take full advantage of the positive press as demand exceeded supply. By the following year, however, production reached its stride and Triumph had an unquestioned success on hand.

The TR2 soon proved itself in competition, gaining an outright win in the RAC Rally, a Coupe des Alpes and the Team Prize in the Alpine Rally, not to mention an impressive fifteenth overall at the 24 Hours of Le Mans, which it achieved while averaging an astounding 35 mpg. It soon developed a reputation as a giant killer, capable of defeating faster and more expensive competition under the right circumstances. Best of all, it was a remarkably practical sports car, offering good fuel economy, impressive storage space and even reasonable comfort for hardy souls. In short, the Triumph was a sports car for all seasons.

Despite strong initial sales through 1954, many customers complained about the excessive exhaust noise, handling and ride concerns, and brake issues, causing sales to slow in the autumn and the following year. Establishing a precedent that would reoccur through the lifespan of the TR range, Triumph improved the car incrementally, as much as it could afford with the minimal funds on hand.

The TR3, introduced at the 1955 London Motor Show at Earls Court, addressed many of the concerns that had been raised against its predecessor. Under the bonnet, modified intake ports and larger 1.75-inch SU carburettors increased the engine's output to 95 bhp at 4,800 rpm, while the available torque rose to 117 pound-feet at 5,000 rpm. For those wanting even more speed, a special Le Mans high-port cylinder head with semi-spherical combustion chambers pushed the power to 100 bhp for not much more cost to the bottom line.

Ken Richardson behind the wheel of a very early production TR2 with long doors. Note the absence of a tonneau cover and the simplified overriders compared to those fitted to 20TS. (Graham Robson Collection)

The TR2 assembly line at Canley during the first year of production. Note the export stickers on the windscreens and Standard Eights in the background. Although most of the TR2s built were sent overseas, declining demand in late 1954 and early 1955 created greater availability in the home market. (Graham Robson Collection)

Externally, a new grill appeared in the void that allowed air into the engine compartment and more brightwork was added to the body. An occasional rear seat was made an option for the cabin, allowing very small children and adults without lower limbs to be carried for short distances, and contrasting colour piping was added to the upholstery.

In spite of greater competition from MG, which had replaced the rather hidebound TF with the modern MGA, Triumph's new model reversed the trend of declining sales and was produced in ever increasing numbers. Late in 1956, Triumph became the first manufacturer to offer disc brakes on a British mass production sports car when it adopted Girling 11-inch front disc brakes as

A technician weighing the frame for the second prototype at the Banner Lane factory. Although some minor modifications would be made over the coming months, this basic chassis would underpin an entire generation of Triumph sports cars. By this time, however, any similarities with the original Flying Eight chassis had long since disappeared. (Graham Robson Collection)

This TR3 with special see-through bodywork was built for the 1956 London Motor Show and subsequently appeared at a number of other events around the country as a promotional tool. (Graham Robson Collection)

standard equipment. Although the Austin-Healey 100S and Jensen 541R had such units on all four wheels, those were produced in such minimal quantities that no one argued when Triumph claimed the distinction in advertisements to help push sales. At the same time, other improvements appeared in the form of a more efficient cylinder head that offered an additional 5 bhp, a sturdier rear axle and revised suspension tuning.

Not content to leave well enough alone, Triumph introduced the TR3A in late 1957, although the new designation was an unofficial one, since management considered it just the latest version of the existing model. Although the mechanical formula was largely unchanged, it looked like a different car with a full-width grille and recessed headlights, not to mention practical improvements

A 1957 TR3 finished in Winchester blue over red. From Commission Number TS13046 in late 1956, front disc brakes were introduced that made the TR3 the first British sports car produced in volume to feature this desirable feature. At the same time Girling rear drum brakes were fitted in the same 10-inch size as before, with more robust half-shafts and redesigned hubs.

This 1956 example is fitted with optional rear wheel spats to lend a sporting look to the profile. These can only be used in conjunction with steel disc wheels.

27

The instrument panel of the TR3 was fundamentally unchanged from the previous model. The steering wheel is an aftermarket item supplied by Moto-Lita in period. Note the remote control for the Laycock de Normanville overdrive on the far left of the fascia.

The occasional rear seat with contrasting piping shown in a 1962 TR3B. Due to the height of the cushion it is only suitable for use with small children.

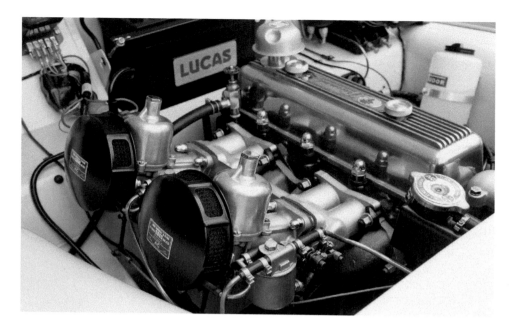

The engine compartment from a 1959 TR3A, showing the SU H6 carburettors that, along with the high-port cylinder head, allowed the 1,991cc unit to produce 100 bhp. The valve cover is a period correct accessory that featured an enamel badge between the knurled nuts.

The TR3B engine shown here was the same 2,138cc unit fitted to the contemporary TR4. The first 500 examples in the TSF Commission Number series had the original 1,991cc powerplant installed, but the later cars had the larger displacement engine fitted. The air cleaners and valve cover are aftermarket accessories.

The primary way to identify the TR3 is the aluminium grille fitted almost flush with the surrounding bodywork. The grille opening was surrounded by chrome moulding, as shown here. Compare the position of the TR3 headlights on the front panel with their recessed position on the TR3A and TR3B.

The TR3A introduced a full width grille that significantly altered the existing appearance without a significant increase in tooling costs. Note that the headlights are slightly recessed into the front panel and that the same badge is used as before but with blue and white replacing the black and red used previously.

such as external door handles and a locking boot as standard equipment, though they had been previously available as part of the optional GT kit. It was also a more comfortable car, with improved seats and side curtains that promised to leak less in the rain than those used before.

In substance, the changes that begat the TR3A were relatively minor, but Triumph was able to sell 58,309 examples, compared to 13,377 units for the TR3. The motoring press appreciated the revised styling and expressed pleasure that the dynamic excellence remained as good as before, noting also that the assembly quality seemed better as well.

Even as the fuel rationing imposed in the wake of the 1956 Suez Canal crisis depressed sales at home, demand continued unabated across the Atlantic, which pushed production to unprecedented levels through the end of the decade. Even in the midst of this success, however, storm clouds were gathering on the

A TR3 body being lowered onto a rolling chassis. At this time the chassis was wheeled along manually from station to station. This primitive operation was replaced during the summer of 1958, when a more modern elevated track was installed that made it possible to increase the pace of production considerably. (Graham Robson Collection)

The bodies for the sidescreen Triumphs were fabricated, trimmed and painted at Mulliners in Birmingham, which was purchased by Standard-Triumph in 1958. The finished bodies were then transported by lorry to Canley for mating with the rolling chassis and sorting out the details. (Graham Robson Collection)

A handsome TR3A painted in powder blue. It is fitted with the optional hardtop and the later style sidescreen with a fixed bottom section and sliding window.

There is little to distinguish this 1962 TR3B from an earlier TR3A. The grille features a slight dish and the headlight rims are wider than those used on all but the last TR3As sold in the United States. Built to alleviate concerns that Americans would shun the TR4 as too modern and expensive, Triumph built only 3,334 examples, all but the first 500 with the larger 2,138cc engine and fully synchronised gearbox.

horizon as the competition began to encroach upon the TR3A's performance advantage and exceed it in terms of refinement and comfort.

The Sunbeam Alpine, Porsche 356 and Alfa Romeo Giulietta boasted roll-up windows and more comfortable interiors, while Austin-Healey and MG were raising the performance stakes with the 100-Six and MGA Twin-Cam. Little could be done to improve the passenger accommodations, but better performance was possible with the 2,138cc engine that was made an option in 1959. First used on the 1958 Alpine Rally cars, it used a larger 86 mm bore to increase the displacement, increasing power by a slight amount in the process.

The familiar Triumph badge on a 1958 TR3A. Vehicles built after January 1959 featured the same item in blue and white, rather than the red and black that had been used since the TR2.

The iconic Lucas P700 headlight was available as an option from 1955, becoming standard equipment in the home market during the following year.

The raised hood on a 1959 TR3A. This example has the sidescreen with fixed bottom fitted. The metal studs reveal the position of the interior securing strap.

This 1958 TR3A displays the later style combined brake lamp with the separate indicator lamp visible at the centre of the frame.

This attractive 1959 TR3A is fitted with chrome wire wheels and an aftermarket exhaust tip. Viewed from this angle the TR3 possesses a profile reminiscent of the Jaguar XK120 but with sharper edges at the rear.

For some time, the TR3B was sold alongside its replacement at Triumph dealers in North America. Because Canley had already commenced with TR4 production, these special models were assembled at the Forward Radiator Co. This Triumph subsidiary also manufactured the body panels using the tooling that had previously been used by Mulliners, another firm in the Standard-Triumph family.

There were hopes that the 'Sabrina' 20X engine that had been developed for the TR3S Le Mans cars could be adapted for series production, but the complex dual overhead camshafts, larger dimensions and higher manufacturing costs put those plans to rest as the company focused its efforts on developing something more modern.

With an economic recession in the United States and Europe during the summer of 1960, however, sales slowed alarmingly, forcing management to push forward plans for the TR3A's replacement. It was the worst timing possible as Triumph was on the brink of financial disaster, caused by having to settle warranty claims for the Herald, pay for a new factory at Canley and tool up for production of the TR4 at the same time.

The tractor business had been sold off to Massey-Ferguson for cash in 1959, but even the £12.5 million received from the sale was not enough to pay for all the company's outstanding obligations. As the smallest of the five largest UK auto manufacturers, behind BMC, Ford, Rootes and Vauxhall, Triumph lacked the necessary economies of scale to turn a consistent profit and the absence of ready capital made it difficult to weather the occasional financial downturn.

Merger talks with Rover, which had occurred several times over the preceding decade, went nowhere, making it clear by late 1960 that Triumph would have to find another suitor and do so soon to stave off disaster. Salvation appeared in the form of Leyland Motors, which had long sought to expand beyond the commercial vehicles that it had built the firm around.

The takeover was announced to the public in April 1961. While the deal ensured Triumph's short-term survival, it was not without consequences and problems. Leyland issued an immediate moratorium on capital projects, principally the TR4 and Spitfire, and then demanded the wholesale resignation or retirement of the existing board of directors.

The situation improved somewhat when the new masters approved the plan to bring both new sports car models to market and allocated enough resources to ensure their initial success. With the TR4 scheduled for release towards the end of 1961, however, it was becoming increasingly difficult to clear the excess inventory of TR3As, but that situation changed once the American dealers caught wind of the new design.

Derided by some powerful dealers in the north-east as too soft and too expensive for customers that had been accustomed to the masculine TR3A, they demanded permission to order the outgoing model alongside its replacement. Retroactively known as the TR3B, 2,801 examples of the last 3,331 TR3s were fitted with the 2,138cc engine and fully synchronized transmission from the TR4 to create the ultimate version of the original TR. These final TCF series cars would close the book on the first real Triumph sports cars. Production for the sidescreen models from the TR2 to TR3B totalled 83,123 units, but the story that they had started would continue, written by thousands of their worthy successors and enthusiastic owners.

Chapter 3
Italian Style

Despite the TR3's strong sales, Triumph started to plan for a successor back in 1956, hoping that it could reach market within three years. With Walter Belgrove having departed during the previous year, the first proposals were created under the watch of Vic Hammond in the Styling Studio. His first efforts were merely mild updates of the current design, featuring hidden headlamps and trim differences. Unhappy with this direction, Hammond abandoned the TR3's bulldog visage and penned a shape that was thoroughly modern and quite attractive. The first mock-up of this design appeared in early 1957, revealing a shape that bore an uncanny resemblance to the Scaglietti-designed Ferrari 250 GT LWB California Spyder.

As undeniably attractive as Hammond's effort was, Triumph had, around the same time, connected with Giovanni Michelotti, who was working on a private commission for Captain Ray Flowers, who was working on developing an indigenous automotive industry in Egypt. Boasting that he was working with a designer who could complete a prototype design from start to finish in ninety days, Triumph executives asserted that such could not be true, but if it were Flowers would be reimbursed for the work.

When the finished car appeared on time and under budget, Triumph was eager to meet the unknown designer, but Flowers demanded to act as an intermediary to maintain control. After some detective work from Martin Tustin and Harry Webster, Triumph's general manager and engineering director respectively, they determined that the impresario was Giovanni Michelotti, who had already gained a reputation as a burgeoning genius. Although still in his mid-thirties, the Italian designer had already developed an impressive portfolio, working on styling commissions for Allemano, Bertone, Ghia and Vignale.

Michelotti had first developed his skills as an apprentice with Stabilimenti Farina, before beginning his long independent association with Vignale, where he styled important variants for the Ferrari 166, 212, 225, 250 and 340 series. He also had some experience with British sports cars, having penned bespoke coachwork for various Austin-Healey and MG models on behalf of Ghia-Aigle in Switzerland. Beyond his obvious brilliance as an automotive stylist, Michelotti worked fast, particularly when inspired, and his fees were considered extremely reasonable, both characteristics that would endear him dearly to the management at Triumph.

Back to the Drawing Board
His first assignment was along the lines of an audition, styling a so-called 'dream car' based on the TR3 to determine if the existing platform could serve as the basis for a new design. Almost alone among the work performed during his long association with Triumph, Michelotti's dream car was poorly integrated

Michelotti built his 'Dream Car' on a TR3 chassis and it is one of the worst examples of his work. With many styling cues cribbed from contemporary American designs, this was nothing more than a styling exercise intended to showcase what was possible from the existing platform. Thankfully, almost every other Michelotti design for Triumph would prove attractive and memorable. (Graham Robson Collection)

The Michelotti Dream Car sits next to Vic Hammond's mock-up in the Styling Studio in 1957. It is likely that the contemporary Ferrari 250 California and other Pinin Farina designs inspired Hammond's work. It is interesting to compare this with Michelotti's Zest and Zoom prototypes. (British Sports Car Hall of Fame)

and relied on too many gimmicks, resembling a smaller version of the Ford Thunderbird, replete with massive grille, sharp tail fins and duotone livery. Still, it was visually arresting, cost just £3,000 to build, was delivered on time, and created a stir among the attendees at the 1957 Geneva Auto Salon.

All things considered, it was a successful trial, and Michelotti was soon offered an informal arrangement to work on several upcoming projects, including a Vanguard saloon update and the design for what would become the Herald. It was his outstanding work on the latter commission that cemented Michelotti's relationship with Triumph. Working with Harry Webster at his Turin base, the small car's final design was sketched out during a single evening and the three prototypes in coupé, saloon and estate versions were completed for only £10,000, thanks to his strong relationship with Vignale.

It would take some time before Michelotti's considerable talents would be directed towards a new TR. Due to lingering uncertainty about the direction to pursue with a replacement for the iconic TR3, it would be some months before Michelotti started work on the project. Being Triumph, there were financial considerations to consider, but much of the debate surrounded the potential use of the 20X dual overhead camshaft engine under development for the Le Mans program. With pronounced camshaft covers, the unit acquired the 'Sabrina' nickname to honour a buxom film star, but despite the cheeky moniker it had the performance to lead the class.

From the moment that it debuted in August 1961, Triumph proved that it could improve upon its original formula in grand fashion. The Michelotti styling was both handsome and masculine, while providing previously unknown levels of comfort with its curved windscreen, rollup windows and wider cabin. Triumph turned the market on its ear with the civilised new roadster at a time when the Austin-Healey 3000 and MGA still offered primitive weather equipment and spartan accommodations.

From this angle the similarities between the TR4 and Zoom prototypes are clear. This 1963 example is finished in a traditional Triumph racing green over black livery. The same exterior colour was also sometimes referred to as conifer.

The displacement increase for the 2,138cc engine was achieved with 86 mm pistons and matching wet cylinder liners. With standard 9.0:1 compression it could produce 105 bhp at 4,600 rpm and 126 pound-feet of torque at 3,350 rpm. Despite the nominal increase in power over the TR3A, the TR4 was not noticeably faster, but it was a far more civilised and practical automobile.

This 1964 TR4 engine is fitted with dual Zenith-Stromberg 175 CD carburettors and a recirculating breather system. With BMC controlling SU, Triumph wanted to form a relationship with independently owned Zenith-Stromberg. The first cars equipped with the 175CD appeared in late 1962 and were in widespread use by the following summer. The SU carburettors would reappear for a time with the TR4A.

Significantly advanced beyond the Vanguard-based pushrod engine used since the 20TS, the Sabrina featured a unique and somewhat complicated cast-iron and alloy sandwich construction engine block. In theory, the four-cylinder unit was cable of producing 160 to 200 bhp from the 1,985cc displacement, which also boasted a robust five-main bearing crankshaft for optimal reliability at high revolutions.

The unit's primary drawbacks were that it was larger than the Vanguard engine and the sandwich block was expensive and difficult to manufacture in mass quantities. The first examples were installed in a trio of racers based on the TR3A, built on lengthened chassis to accommodate the larger powerplant. Although none of the cars finished their competition debut at the 1959 24 Hours of Le Mans, the Sabrina showed enough promise for management to consider its use for the TR road car.

Although it was built upon the narrower TR3A chassis, Michelotti's Zest prototype previewed many of the styling elements that would appear in the TR4. Almost the entire styling forward of the windscreen was retained in some fashion, although the bonnet bulge was smoothed into a teardrop shape. (Graham Robson Collection)

The most attractive of the Michelotti designs was probably the first of the two Zoom prototypes. Built on a wheelbase that was 6 inches longer to accommodate the Sabrina engine, it was also widened for better handling and more interior space. Much of the styling from behind the windscreen was translated for use on the TR4. (Graham Robson Collection)

Finally provided with some direction, dimensions and potential hard points to plan around, Michelotti started on the TR3A's replacement. His first effort received the Zest code name and was built on a standard narrow chassis. It featured prominent headlamp eyelids, an Italianate profile and a curvaceous bonnet with a prominent bulge to clear the carburettor dashpots, all features that became TR4 hallmarks.

Around the same time, Michelotti had also designed an attractive coupé body for use with the TR3A's chassis and running gear. Shown at the 1958 Turin Auto Show, it received significant attention and popular acclaim, allowing the Italian designer to sell it as the Triumph Italia 2000 from 1959 to 1962. The 329 examples were built at Vignale on rolling chassis shipped from Coventry and were originally intended as a semi-sanctioned model that would have been sold through Triumph dealers in North America. Leyland's takeover in 1961 put an end to those plans, forcing Triumph's Italian distributors to market the car through various small importers in the United States, although some later examples were sold through authorised Standard-Triumph franchises.

Most importantly, the Italia's styling influenced Michelotti's Zoom prototypes, which followed the Zest in a continuing attempt to find the next TR. Built on an extended TR3A frame to accommodate the larger Sabrina, the track was also widened to provide better road holding and increase interior room, which were known deficiencies with the existing model. The wider frame also made it possible to add rack and pinion steering, an important advantage since most of the TR3A's competitors still had cam and peg units.

Introduced at the 1958 Turin Auto Show, Michelotti used a number of styling themes for the 2000 Italia that would also appear in his Zoom prototypes. A second prototype appeared at Turin the year after, more closely resembling the production versions, which by then were already under construction at Vignale. At a $5,000 purchase price for a car powered by the running gear from the humble TR3A, sales were slower than expected, forcing production to a halt after 329 examples were built.

Although the instruments and switchgear were sourced from the Triumph parts bin, the presentation and layout were absolutely first-rate.

The interior appointments were on par with contemporary Italian sports cars and featured thicker seat cushions, wool carpets, and leather-trimmed surfaces throughout the cabin.

From this view it is simple to see the similarities between the 2000 Italia and the Zoom prototypes. By extension, this styling was also carried through the TR4 and its successors. Even the front wing profile seems to have influenced the TR6.

While the doors and rear end resembled the Zest, the styling forward of the firewall was much smoother and simpler, displaying uncovered headlamps and a smaller grille aperture, hinting at the Ferrari 250 GT Cabriolet. In the end, Michelotti constructed two versions of the Zoom formula to test various styling cues, both similar to the Italia, but differing from one another in frontal details.

The Emperor's New Clothes

With two Michelotti-penned shapes to consider, management decided to back the Zoom concept. In order to test the public's response to this dramatic styling departure, Triumph decided to duplicate the Zoom's shape in fiberglass to mate with the chassis and running gear from the previous year's Le Mans entrants, allowing the old TR3S to become the new TRS. With the 1960 24 Hours of Le Mans around the corner, Triumph could give the assembled masses a sneak preview of the upcoming TR4 and gain valuable publicity from the motoring press.

Even before these attractive racing cars had arrived on French shores, however, Triumph had second thoughts about the choice that had been made. In a familiar refrain, the company's financial condition had grown precarious due to increasing warranty claims, outstanding capital obligations and the looming spectre of significant tooling costs for the new TR4. With time to think about these looming expenditures, management got cold feet about their flagship's future. It seemed that a merger was on the horizon, and not wanting to commit to such a wholesale revision, Triumph waffled, committing to new bodywork and some comfort improvements, but leaving the longer chassis and twin-cam powerplant on the shelf.

Just like that, plans for the Sabrina's use in the TR4 were abandoned, which obviated the need for the lengthened Zoom chassis, though it was later shown that the standard frame could have accommodated the more powerful unit

The TR4 rolling chassis was basically similar to that used by the outgoing TR3A, but note the rack and pinion steering and the front and rear track, which are 4 inches wider. There has also been an additional resonator installed aft of the rear axle. (Graham Robson Collection)

without problem. Instead, Michelotti was asked to combine the best elements from his two styling proposals. The Zoom inspired the styling from the windscreen aft, while the forward profile, including the bonnet, came from the Zest. Beneath the skin were the wider track and rack and pinion steering from the extended frame, while the TR3A's venerable pushrod powerplant would carry forward, but in a slightly larger 2,138cc displacement.

Having decided on an amalgam of Michelotti's competing designs, Triumph moved fast to advance the new car towards production. Making things more difficult on this front was the Leyland management's decision to suspend any further capital outlays, which put the TR4 and the upcoming Spitfire on ice. After understanding the importance of both sports car projects to the company's future, Leyland relented, allowing the car to enter the final stages of the production process.

The first seats fitted to the TR4 were almost the same as those used on the TR3A. A new style seat appeared after Body Number 15076 CT that had a rectangular lower cushion and flatter backrest. The walnut veneer dashboard was available as an option on left-hand drive examples from late 1963, before becoming standard equipment on the TR4A and the final examples of the TR4.

This 1965 TR4A interior features seats that are very different from those seen in the previous photograph. The seatback displays more pronounced curvature and the lower cushion has radiused corners with supportive bolstering around the outer edge. The Moto-Lita steering wheel is a period correct accessory but the radio and auxiliary ashtray are more modern additions.

Early TR4 examples featured this attractive metal dash that was painted in either spa or new white. The centre panel housing the minor instruments was alternately finished in turned aluminium or black crackle paint. With so many dashes converted to wood veneer, the painted version depicted here is a rare sight. Note the fresh air vent at the left, which was a first in a car of this type.

The TR4 and TR4A featured a generous boot with unsurpassed practicality for a sports car. Because the spare tire was housed in a recess under the floor panel it kept luggage and other contents free from dirt or rubber residue. The fuel tank is located behind the vertical cardboard panel. Later model TR4s and the TR4As were equipped with an automatic stay for the boot lid, as shown here.

The TR3A chassis was carried over to reduce costs, although the front track was increased by 4 inches to facilitate mounting the Alford & Alder steering rack. At the rear, no modifications were needed, as lengthened half-shafts and axle tubes made up the difference in width, although the problem with restricted rear wheel movement persisted. With the bodyshell mounted as a single unit on the chassis, the TR4 was more rigid. Despite this, the suspension felt more compliant, thanks to revised damper settings, additional weight and unchanged spring rates.

Under the bonnet resided the familiar Vanguard unit in 2,138cc form, which had been available as an option with the previous model. The previous 1,991cc engine remained available at no cost to allow competition in 2-litre racing classes. Although the rated horsepower of the larger engine remained the same at 100 bhp, increased compression and a revised camshaft profile liberated more actual power. A redesigned gearbox provided synchromesh on all forward gears, which was an important feature considering that the Austin-Healey 3000 and MGA still had unsynchronized first gears. An electric overdrive manufactured by Laycock de Normanville remained available as an option.

Pressed and assembled on the outskirts of Liverpool in Speke, the new bodies were delivered as complete shells on special transporters for assembly at Canley. In addition to the obvious visual appeal of Michelotti's design, it also allowed for far more comfort than was possible from the TR3A.

The TR4 production line at Canley. The wooden bumpers were fitted to facilitate stowage aboard ships bound for export markets. Note that these examples are almost certainly destined for overseas sale as they feature left-hand steering. (Graham Robson Collection)

47

The addition of roll-up windows and a curved windscreen transformed the passenger cabin into a space that could remain dry even in inclement weather, while the wider dimensions provided an additional 2½ inches for hips and shoulders. The new bodyshell also paid unexpected dividends, such as three more inches for legroom and more spacious accommodations for the poor souls that had to endure the occasional rear seat.

The full-width dashboard contained the same instruments as before, but for the first time in a British car incorporated unique face-level vents that could direct fresh air into the cabin through an intake mounted in front of the windscreen.

Another Michelotti innovation was the two-piece hardtop, featuring a fixed alloy casting for the backlight and a removable centre section to allow for open air motoring with less wind buffeting in the cockpit. The ingenious design debuted on the TR3 Dream Car and appeared again on the Zoom prototypes. In the TR4, the removable pressed steel panel could be replaced, as an option, with a lighter vinyl substitute, hence the Surrey top name, which eventually came to identify the entire hardtop structure. Although it was expensive, and thus seldom ordered, it nonetheless represented a significant design achievement, which Porsche and Fiat would use to great advantage over the coming years.

Whether the TR4 was more attractive than the Zoom prototypes or Victor Hammond's initial styling exercise is subject to debate, but it was certainly an improvement over the TR3A and compared well against its rivals. Despite fears from some dealers that it was too much a departure from the rough-hewn sidescreen models, the TR4 was an immediate success.

The first car was manufactured on 18 July 1961, with the new model getting its public debut in September. By the end of the year, 2,648 units had been delivered to waiting customers, but fewer than a dozen to owners in Britain. Over the first full year of production, 15,956 units were built, falling short of the TR3A's record in 1959, but a strong showing in a market that had become far more competitive. While the TR4 would certainly have benefitted from more power and a revised suspension, both the public and press were generally enthusiastic, praising its comfort and performance.

The Motor appreciated the improvements, but complained that the aging chassis reduced the value of the new package:

Compact dimensions and an excellent engine and gearbox enable the TR4 to offer more performance than any other production sports car at the price. The body is practical, convenient and roomy; if the chassis design could be brought up to the same standard as the rest, the car would undoubtedly command an even greater share of the sports car market than it does already.

The conclusion that Triumph could have done more with the TR4 was a sentiment shared by many. During the financial crisis that led to the Leyland takeover, management had been forced to abandon the new chassis when the Zoom design was rejected, although some of the existing faults could be traced to the speed with which the model was brought to market.

Inspired by the Harrington Alpine, the Dove GTR4 could have obviated the need for the MGB GT had it been produced in volume. The handsome fastback coupé was sold and named after L. F. Dove, Triumph's distributor in Wimbledon. Built in very small numbers by Thomas Harrington & Company, it was too expensive to make an impact on the market. Of course, series production would likely have brought the costs down to a reasonable figure, leading one to wonder what could have been. (Graham Robson Collection)

Triumph began to address some of these issues as soon it could. Within six months the front suspension geometry was improved, which was achieved by changing the castor angle from zero to 3° through modifying the design of the top ball joint and trunnion. At the same time, smaller and lighter front brake callipers appeared and later that year came more comfortable seats, featuring new frames and cushions, establishing the basic shape that would remain until the TR6 arrived on the scene.

The MGB and Austin-Healey 3000 Mk II that appeared in 1962 dampened enthusiasm for the TR4 to a certain extent, but the model's blend of performance, comfortable accommodations and practicality allowed it to continue to sell well in the face of the increased competition. In reality, the biggest threat to its future success was an internal one, stemming from the TR4's compromised chassis layout, which road testers pointed out at every possible opportunity.

Road & Track, America's most influential automotive publication, wrote:

On a smooth surface, the road holding is very good and there is little or no body lean, but on poor surfaces the very limited movement of the suspension becomes apparent, and the back tends to hop and will bottom out quite easily on a severe bump. The rear suspension is our major criticism, and we felt that the whole car would be greatly improved if the rear end was updated.

49

Critical Response

With potential customers reading these reviews, Triumph needed to respond to preserve market share. Ever since the 20TS, engineers had realised that the original rear suspension design was compromised because it allowed the axle to contact the frame as it moved vertically, preventing the rear wheels from maintaining contact with the road. The problem was not the solid axle and leaf spring arrangement, since it was the same system used by other sports car manufacturers, including the Alfa Romeo, Austin-Healey and MG, but the Triumph's layout allowed for a smaller range of motion, causing the rear end to 'dance and skitter' on rough surfaces.

Triumph had wanted a fully revised suspension in 1962, though financial problems at the time scuttled the plan. The most expedient solution was to retrofit an independent rear suspension (IRS) to the old frame, since it would answer the clamour from the critics while placing the TR4 in a better position vis-à-vis the competition, which also used live rear axles.

Importantly, Triumph was no stranger to IRS, using fully independent suspensions for the Herald, Spitfire and Vitesse. Adopting a similar arrangement for the TR4 was problematic, however, since the rear frame would need

A 1966 TR4A finished in a highly attractive Wedgewood blue over midnight blue colour scheme. This example is fitted with a live rear axle that was made available over concerns that certain American customers would be unwilling to pay the extra cost associated with IRS.

The attractive profile of a 1966 TR4A IRS fitted with the Surrey top. The fixed backlight is easily distinguished due to the contrasting colour of the removable hard centre section.

This 1966 TR4A is fitted with Stromberg 175 CD carburettors and the correct style air filters for this application. The chrome finish on the valve cover and the eared filler cap are correct. There was no performance difference between engines fitted with the SU and Zenith-Stromberg carburettors, although some tuning experts suggest that the flexible diaphragm in the latter allows for more precise operation. The inlet manifold shown here was fitted with both carburettor versions and is universally considered the best performing among the five manifold variants used for the TR2-4A. Note the PCV valve located between the inlet manifold and valve cover.

This 1963 TR4 is fitted with the Surrey top and magnesium alloy wheels, which were a desirable feature for competition examples. Note the pressed aluminium grille containing both turn indicators and running lights. The overriders on the TR4 are much closer together than the smaller items fitted to the TR4A.

substantial modifications to mount the new components and allow them the required clearance. Compounding the problem, several important dealers in the United States demanded that the solid rear axles be retained as an option for customers that lived in states where smooth and straight roads predominated, fearful that they would refuse to pay for such an unnecessary extravagance. Accommodating this position meant that Triumph would have to produce a chassis frame that could work with both rear suspension alternatives, increasing the difficulty of the task.

Unlike the crude and inexpensive swing-axle arrangement used in the Herald, Vitesse and Spitfire, scorned by most for its dangerous propensity towards snap oversteer, Triumph wisely chose to adopt a more sophisticated semi-trailing arm and coil spring design. This eliminated the tendency to change camber radically when the rear end unloaded during cornering that hamstrung Triumph's small car trio.

The general layout, if not the actual components themselves, came from the design used for Triumph's 2000 saloon. Introduced in 1963 with striking Michelotti coachwork, it was an upmarket replacement for the Standard Vanguard, which had helped to reverse the company's fortunes as it emerged from the austerity measures imposed by Leyland just a few years earlier.

To adapt the 2000's rear suspension, engineers designed a new bell-shaped chassis, where the cast aluminium semi-trailing arms pivoted on the chassis frame with a single coil spring on each arm, attached to a transverse bridge that also supported the differential casing. Due to the TR4's space restrictions, the 2000's telescopic shock absorbers were replaced with archaic hydraulic lever arm dampers, but this had a minimal effect on handling. For the live axle cars, bound for penny-pinching American customers, almost half of whom lived in the north-east, the bridge piece was omitted, with the leaf springs and brackets mounted directly to the frame.

With the addition of the improved rear suspension, it was obvious that a new model would herald the introduction to boost sales. As the final specification for the TR4A was being discussed, proposals were weighed to introduce a more powerful engine along with the improved suspension. There had been talk about installing a six-cylinder unit, but the available options were not much of an improvement over the existing 2,138cc powerplant.

Increasing the displacement of the old four-cylinder engine was also considered, since the cylinder liners could be removed to create a dry version

The pressed aluminium grille used in the TR4 was replaced with a more modern assembly with horizontal bars for the TR4A. For whatever reason a hole remains at the bottom of the grille for a starting handle despite the absence of a hole in the radiator to reach the crankshaft snout.

The TR4A received a new chrome assembly mounted on the front wing that contained the side lamp and turn signal indicator light. A bright trim strip ran from the housing to the doors along the character line stamped in the body panel.

with a displacement of 2,499cc, but after some prototypes were tested it seemed that not enough power was gained to make the change worthwhile. As it was, changes to the camshaft profile and an improved exhaust increased horsepower slightly to 104 bhp at 4,700 rpm, while the available torque increased to 132 pound-feet at 3,000 rpm. This modest gain was offset by the increased weight from the revised frame and suspension, meaning that performance was much the same as before.

There were other improvements beyond IRS, however, including revised front suspension geometry that raised the front roll centre to improve turn-in response, a wider radiator with better cooling capacity, a more robust diaphragm clutch that lowered the reciprocating mass, and a simple fixed assembly hood that could be erected in far less time than the old unit. Inside the cabin, the walnut dashboard that had recently been introduced for American models was made available worldwide and revised seats with improved cushioning and more rake provided more comfort. External changes were limited to a new grille, revised badges and the relocation of the sidelights and indicators to a chromed housing on the front fenders, which was accompanied by additional brightwork leading aft to the doors.

The TR4A was well received by the press, and critics of the previous solid axle arrangement were gratified that Triumph had listened to their complaints. *Autocar* happily reported that 'the TR can be driven deliberately fast at obstacles it would have shied away from before', while another publication in America proclaimed 'the new suspension is also little short of remarkable'.

Appreciated for more than its new rear suspension, the TR4A was a more refined vehicle, but retained the robust character that had distinguished its forebears. As related in a road test from *Car and Driver*, 'As a package it stands as one of the most satisfactory automobiles available today. It still has that marvellous reliability, even more than previously, and will pound down the road at high speeds for hours on end without showing any signs of tiring.'

The first TR4A was completed on 5 January 1965 and met a market that was eager for its introduction. Sales on both sides of the Atlantic remained strong throughout its life, slowing only when rumours of an imminent replacement were rife. During its first year on sale, the TR4A surpassed the TR4's sales record from the previous two, but it would enjoy a relatively short time in the sun. Produced from January 1965 to July 1967, only 28,468 examples were built, with almost 21,000 shipped to North America.

Around one-third of the cars sold in the United States were equipped with the live rear axle, justifying the insistence of certain dealers to retain it. Running changes were limited to the replacement of the Zenith-Stromberg 175 CD carburettors, which had first appeared in 1963, with SU HS6 units, and the later adoption of a single outlet exhaust system.

A successful model, with strong sales and increased appreciation from the press, the TR4A arrived in changing times for the global sports car market. In comparative terms, although having remained stagnant for quite some time,

This photograph from 2 August 1967 shows the final TR4A rolling off the assembly line in front of the first TR250 bound for America. (Graham Robson Collection)

the TR4A's performance remained in the same ballpark as the Austin-Healey 3000 Mk III and remained superior to the MGB and Sunbeam Alpine. But those hallowed names no longer represented the primary competition. Exceptional, affordable sports cars from Alfa Romeo, Datsun, Fiat, Porsche and Volvo were now part of the equation, as were an increasing number of sports sedans from a host of manufacturers, particularly in the American market where the Mustang scavenged numerous customers.

Especially in Europe, where new motorway construction made driving at sustained speeds more practicable, it was becoming more difficult to remain competitive with only 14 more horsepower than was available from the TR2. Even worse, Federal pollution and safety regulations that were appearing over the American horizon threatened future performance in unimagined ways. For survival in this environment, Triumph would have to abandon the Vanguard-based powerplant that had served the TR well since 1952. Fortunately, management was aware of the dilemma and was already working on a solution.

Chapter 4
The Wonder Twins

The short-lived siblings, the TR5 and TR250, were born from indecision about what should be done to address the issue of the TR's moribund performance and concern over the evolving regulatory climate in the United States regarding pollution.

For once, this dilemma was addressed from a position of relative strength, rather than having to labour under severe financial restrictions. Total unit sales were approaching unprecedented levels, and each new model that was introduced during the 1960s had met with enthusiastic demand. Throughout the decade, the company had capitalised on the public's increasing appetite for performance cars, kindled by vehicles like the Mini Cooper and Ford Cortina. Beyond the TR, Triumph could offer the Spitfire, Vitesse, GT6 and 2000 saloon to the automotive enthusiast, but the stagnant performance of the flagship needed improvement to maintain the company's credibility as a performance marque.

There was little doubt that the output from the venerable four-cylinder engine had been pushed as far as it could without threatening the reliability for which it had become famous. Every attempt to extract more power from the unit, such as increasing the displacement through dry cylinder walls, met with the harsh reality that the final results were outweighed by the time, expense and effort to achieve them.

Prior to the TR4A's introduction, engineers had considered the 1,998cc six-cylinder engine under development for the Standard Vanguard 6, but declined after realising that it conferred no advantage whatsoever in terms of horsepower (80 bhp at 4,400 rpm) and torque (108 pound-feet at 2,500 rpm) over the old four-cylinder powerplant.

With replacement of the TR4A on the horizon, and having accepted that the old four-cylinder engine was at a developmental dead end, engineers revisited the Vanguard 6 unit. Dating from the late 1940s, it started as an undersquare 803cc four-cylinder unit that was used in the Standard Eight saloon from 1953 to 1959. With more small models on the horizon, such as the Herald and Spitfire, the little engine grew to provide more power. By increasing the bore, the displacement increased to 948cc and then 1,147cc, before eventually expanding to 1,296cc. Further enlargement of the bore and stroke resulted in a final 1,493cc capacity, where it would power the final versions of the MG Midget and Triumph Spitfire.

A unique design, a matter of coincidence rather than intent, the engine was amenable to substantial internal modification. It could also be modified externally, through the addition of extra cylinders tacked on to the block ends. In 1960, using this approach, the four was transformed into a six, where it powered the Vanguard 6, and three years later in the Triumph 2000. Although it was smooth and refined, it was not very powerful, which had doomed its prospects for use in the TR4A.

This prototype began life as a TR4 that was later used as a developmental mule to trial fit the 2-litre six-cylinder engine. The Michelotti styling would undergo several variations, including in later form with hidden headlamps. This was a distant predecessor of the TR6 that had little effect on the final product. (Graham Robson Collection)

This was an internal styling proposal to determine how much of the existing TR4A styling could be retained in a successor. Note the smooth bonnet that would mark similar exercises built around the same time, although the bulge would remain in the TR5/TR250. (Graham Robson Collection)

Nothing more than another example of Michelotti's amazing ability to work under extreme pressure, the TR5 Ginevra was built in barely more than two weeks for the 1968 Geneva Motor Show. The original plan was for Michelotti to display the Stag on his studio's stand, but at the last minute Triumph asked to move it to their own display area. With nothing to exhibit, Michelotti penned this unique design at the last minute and had the finished prototype ready in fifteen days. Rumour has it that the Triumph Fury's body buck was used during its construction. (Francois Borzellino)

The Fury was the first monocoque sports car that Triumph built and featured an amalgam of Michelotti styling themes. With an all-independent suspension and a six-cylinder engine from the 2000 saloon, it would have represented a complete departure from the existing TR range. Reluctant to pursue production of a model that would have been expensive to tool and build, Triumph chose to back the traditional TR5/TR250 instead. (Graham Robson Collection)

Further increasing the bore was not an option as there was not enough space in the block for larger pistons. With no better alternatives, and needing more power, Triumph lengthened the stroke from 76 mm to 95 mm. It was an audacious move, since most performance engines in the 1960s featured oversquare dimensions to enable higher rpms, rather than the stump pulling motors that had dominated in the previous decade.

It was no simple change to effect, making the task more complex, requiring a comprehensive redesign of the crankshaft, connecting rods, pistons, head and the cylinder block. With these modifications in place, however, the displacement increased to 2,498cc, which produced about 110 bhp. Although this wasn't bad, it was a scant improvement over the 104 bhp from the old unit in the TR4A, which did not seem worth all the effort.

A Break With the Past

Management had determined that any new TR engine would need to produce 150 bhp for a desired 120 mph top speed and 0 to 60 mph acceleration under nine seconds. But further attempts to wring out additional performance from the six-cylinder unit reduced refinement and tractability to unacceptable levels.

The solution to this seemingly insoluble problem came in the form of a new mechanical fuel injection system that had been under protracted development by Lucas. The innovative design promised not only better performance, but also increased fuel economy and reduced emissions that could enable compliance with strict pollution regulations that were about to appear in the United States. After fitting the Lucas Mark II system to an engine with a hotter camshaft produced 150 bhp at 5,500 rpm, management were elated, especially since the new cam profile failed to affect drivability due to the unit's precise metering system.

The TR5 PI became the first British production automobile to feature petrol injection when it arrived in 1967, offering performance that distanced itself from the TR's previous rivals from a performance standpoint.

Compelled for various reason to retain the Zenith-Stromberg carburettors for the TR250 sold in the United States, Triumph trumpeted the smoothness made possible by the new 2,498cc six-cylinder engine. 8,484 examples were sold in a production run that spanned fifteen months.

Among the visual differences between the TR5 and TR4A were a new trapezoidal bonnet badge and a matte black finish for the upper surfaces of the horizontal grille slats. Note that the opening for the starting handle disappeared from the grille, though the indentation in the lower valence panel remained.

The new powerplant was installed in the existing engine compartment with little difficulty after the radiator was moved forward to accommodate the longer cylinder block. With an output of 150 hp at 5,500 rpm and 164 pound-feet of torque at 3,500 rpm, power was up by almost 50 per cent over the TR4A, allowing acceleration from 0 to 60 mph in 8.5 seconds. Among the other visible changes under the bonnet were an alternator, brake servo booster, and cooling hoses fashioned from new materials.

It was far too much to ask that a restyled body accompany the new powerplant. Instead, room for the new powerplant came from moving the radiator forward and reworking the chassis cross-braces and engine mounts. To facilitate the 50 per cent increase in power, stronger rear springs, modified trailing arms, radial tires on wider wheels, uprated brakes with servo assistance and a plastic radiator fan were added, along with a higher rear axle ratio. An oil cooler was also made available to prolong engine life under sustained high-speed operation, while an alternator appeared as standard equipment, along with a tandem brake master cylinder with dual circuits to meet new American safety requirements.

Externally, there was little to distinguish between the new models from the TR4A. The power bulge on the hood remained, even though it no longer served a functional purpose. Reversing lamps and rear side marker lights were incorporated into the existing sheet metal, with wider chrome trim used behind the forward light cluster and additional brightwork attached to the outer sills. Matte black paint was added to the horizontal grille slats for a more modern appearance, while an offset trapezoidal badge with the new model designation replaced the familiar globe design.

Although wire wheels remained available, Rostyle wheel covers, mimicking the look of more expensive magnesium alloy wheels, were adopted in a nod to the changed tastes of the period. Evolving safety standards forced most of the interior changes, such as the padded steering wheel spokes, matte dash finish, and safer switchgear and door hardware. There were more warning lights and the ashtray moved to the upper dash pad, but other than circular air vents and revised instrument graphics, the layout remained unchanged. Also added were improved seats with ventilated surfaces and formed cushions that better fit the body.

It was thought that the new fuel injected engine would address the two most pressing issues that Triumph faced with the TR4A's replacement: the moribund performance and the strict American pollution regulations. Providing more precise fuel metering than carburettors, fuel injection was clearly the best option for reducing tailpipe emissions and Alfa Romeo, BMW, Lancia and Porsche all adopted similar systems to meet the same challenge.

Unfortunately, the Lucas design was in its infancy and there was little experience with how the system would fare in daily operation. Most historians have argued that fuel injection was not adopted for the US market because it was incapable of meeting the new standards that were to become effective on 1 January 1968 without undergoing further refinement and expensive modification.

It is far more likely that Triumph was unwilling to introduce this untried technology into its most important market without sufficient confidence that it would operate reliably and could be competently maintained in a vast country with variable access to skilled technicians. Still smarting from the Herald's vast warranty claims, Triumph believed that safe was better than sorry, especially with the TR flagship. Further complicating matters was the issue of expense. American dealers had recently argued that many customers were unwilling to pay for an independent rear suspension; would these same individuals spend the premium required for fuel injection?

The die was cast when engineers were able to meet the exacting new pollution standards with dual Zenith-Stromberg 175 CD carburettors that had undergone strict calibration and were then sealed to prevent tampering, although the idle speed remained adjustable. An expedient and inexpensive solution, the tried and true carburettors were also likely more reliable than the unproven Lucas system. In many ways, Triumph's concerns were later justified when the new layout proved troublesome and hard to maintain for the first few years that it was available.

Regrettably, all the performance that fuel injection offered was lost with the return to carburettors, although the smoothness and torque from the six-cylinder engine was certainly a welcome change. In raw numbers, output from the six-cylinder engine with carburettors was right back where it was before, meaning that a faster TR for the American market remained an unfulfilled promise.

Split Decision

When it became clear that there were to be two distinct versions of the next TR, one for the United States and one for the rest of the world, Triumph decided to identify them separately. The American version would be called the TR250, while the fuel injected model for the rest of the world became the TR5.

Both models would mark the final break with the first sidescreen models. The TR4 had introduced a handsome new body, while the TR4A came with a new chassis and independent rear suspension. The TR250 and TR5 would abandon the old four-cylinder engine that had powered both tractors and sports cars, having been on duty for more than a decade with admirable reliability.

Because the TR250 would have performance roughly equivalent to its predecessors, Triumph sought to mollify disappointed customers with a transverse racing stripe across the bonnet that dealers hoped would make the car appear faster than it actually was. In truth, the TR250 benefitted greatly from the new engine: it was much smoother, more tractable and the additional torque improved the performance, ever so slightly, allowing acceleration from 0 to 60 mph in less than 11 seconds and a 110 mph top speed.

The power bulge that Michelotti incorporated into the TR4 bonnet was an enduring design element. It was rendered superfluous with the adoption of the Lucas Mark II petrol injection system and Zenith-Stromberg carburettors, though it remained until the TR6's introduction.

In the absence of a measurable performance increase, the TR250 resorted to visual gimmicks to provide the impression of speed. With input from Bruce McWilliams, an executive based in the United States, Triumph applied transverse racing stripes across the vehicle's nose and increased the width of the stainless steel trim behind the sidelight cluster.

A badge proclaiming that this example bears the potent Lucas Mark II petrol injection system and the optional Laycock de Normanville overdrive unit.

For the fourth time since the TR4's introduction, Triumph introduced a new seat design. Both the TR5 and TR250 featured 'Embossed Breathing Ambla' as standard equipment although leather was an option, as shown in this TR5. When leather surfaces were ordered the pleats were smooth and free of embossing.

While the refinement from the new engine was a welcome change, it was not enough to satisfy those discouraged at Triumph's decision to withhold the TR5 from the world's largest market. The most scathing rebuke came from *Car and Driver*, who wrote that 'to pay an extra $500 for a nearly identical, but slower car doesn't make much sense'. Customers felt the same way, though most knew that the TR250 was an interim model, destined for replacement not long into the future.

It would be unfair, however, to describe the TR250 as a poor seller, since it found a steady supply of buyers during its brief run. In fact, helped by strong demand for the Spitfire Mk III and GT6, North American dealers reached record numbers during the summer of 1968. Both the TR250 and TR5 would be produced for a shorter period than any other TR, with the former outselling the latter by a healthy margin. The first TR250 was built on 11 July 1967 and the last on 19 September 1968, reaching a final total of 8,484 units.

When the inaugural TR5 was assembled on 29 August 1967, it became the first British production car to feature fuel injection, and its performance placed it in the van among its peers. Expectedly, press reaction to the TR5 was far more positive than the reception that greeted its less powerful brother.

The British motoring press was ebullient about the new model's performance, publishing unabashedly positive reviews right from the start. *Motor*'s evaluation was typical: 'On the basis that high maximum and cruising speeds and vivid acceleration are the essential agreements of a true sports car, this magnificent power unit is the answer to the enthusiast's prayer.'

Despite the TR5's positive press, Triumph had long ago hitched its star to the US market, rendering most other sales secondary, except in the area of saloons and commercial vehicles, where the United Kingdom remained the most important source of customers. In contrast to the 8,484 TR250s sold in North America, only 1,165 TR5s were delivered to British customers. The remaining 1,782 examples were split among France, Germany, Australia, New Zealand and the Far East, though handfuls were scattered in other markets around the globe.

Even as the TR5 and TR250 were entering production, Triumph were well aware they represented an interim solution, intended solely to test the waters with the new engine and fuel injection system, and buying time until plans for an updated body were finalised. It was apparent that the world marketplace was ready for a more modern shape to accompany the improved performance, while the Americans wanted something major to change if the performance could not. But the late 1960s were a turbulent time on many fronts, especially for the British motor industry, which would have a huge impact on Triumph's future in the days to come.

Rationalisation, which had become an important word during the putative merger with Leyland back in 1961, swept through the British automotive industry over the course of the decade. Ford, Rootes and Vauxhall would emerge unscathed for the time being, but BMC, Jaguar and Leyland-Triumph were not as fortunate. Notwithstanding its status as the largest manufacturer in Britain, BMC remained, according to historian Graham Robson, 'a rather loose and uneasy alliance' between Austin and the old Nuffield organization, but it had continued to grow roots in piecemeal fashion over the preceding decade without much regard for profits or operating efficiencies.

The BMC merger with Pressed Steel in 1965, however, would prove to be the tipping point, causing momentous consequences for the future of automotive manufacturing in Britain. Pressed Steel supplied bodies to Jaguar, Rolls-Royce, Rootes, Rover and Standard-Triumph, and while there was never much question that it would continue to do so, the marriage caused concern because no responsible firm wanted to entrust proprietary design materials and production details to an operation that was directly controlled by a rival.

At least Rootes and Standard-Triumph had options, through existing relationships or by developing facilities of their own, but Jaguar, Rolls-Royce and Rover lacked the same wherewithal. In this environment, Jaguar agreed to join BMC to form British Motor Holdings (BMH) in 1966, allowing the small firm access to greater resources. Not long afterwards, in a further rush of merger mania, Leyland-Triumph absorbed Rover. By the time that the TR6 emerged in 1969, the world had changed forever. On 17 January 1968, British Leyland arose from the marriage of BMH and Leyland-Triumph, formerly bitter rivals who would now have to coexist as strange bedfellows. British sports cars would never be the same.

This profile view shows the wider stainless steel trim leading from the sidelight housing and the additional brightwork attached to the sills. A discrete badge was fitted to the rear wing, proclaiming the capacity of the new powerplant under the bonnet.

A number of additional safety requirements were made mandatory in the United States for the 1968 model year, including the white reversing lamps seen in this TR250. The traditional eared knockoff was outlawed and replaced with an octagonal version that was considered safer in an accident, although this example still has the former items installed. Note the TR250 badge on the rear wing in place of the 2500 badge that the TR5 displayed.

Although the 2,498cc six-cylinder engine was smoother and more tractable than the Vanguard-based unit, American customers were disappointed that the performance of the TR250 had not significantly improved despite the displacement increase. Nonetheless, the motoring press appreciated the refinement on hand and called the new model 'a real improvement over the TR4A'.

Like many examples that have had a repaint in the past, this TR250 has lost the racing stripes across the nose that usually distinguish the TR5's American sibling. Note the octagonal knockoff nuts for the wire wheels and white reversing lamp visible under the nearside cathedral taillight cluster.

Chapter 5
Modern Love

As the TR5 and TR250 approached production in 1967, Triumph had already commenced plans for their replacement. Due to design commitments with other Triumph models and Leyland commercial vehicles, Giovanni Michelotti lacked the time to lead the effort. Instead, management had to cast about for a substitute that could perform the work in the short time available and do so for the little money available. After weighing the alternatives, the project was assigned to Wilhelm Karmann GmbH in Osnabrück, Germany, which had established an enviable reputation performing production and design work for American Motors, BMW, Porsche and Volkswagen.

The task was especially arduous, since any new design would have to retain the inner panels, floors, scuttle, doors and windscreen from the previous models, which limited potential changes to the exterior body panels. Even worse, a temporary shortage in British die-making capacity meant that Karmann would also have to produce the manufacturing tools for the new model and do so in time to meet the looming deadlines.

Fortunately, the compressed time frame forced stylist Gerhard Giesecke to focus his attention. Incredibly, Triumph approved Karmann's very first proposal in September 1967, setting the wheels in motion to get the car into production fast. Considering the time and resource restrictions, not to mention the demand to retain the inner structure, what resulted was nothing short of miraculous.

The finished Karmann prototype shows how close it is to the production TR6. Note that this example retains the Michelotti-designed hardtop dating from the TR4 and a unique badge fastened to the trim strip on the grille. (David Knowles)

Described in an early review as 'one of the rare facelift jobs that actually comes off well', the TR6 had an aggressive stance that reeked of virility. Even though nothing had changed under the skin, from the outside it looked like a wholly new design, rather than a superficially reworked TR5/TR250. Through judicious alteration of the front and rear, the aging silhouette was transformed into a modern classic.

With elements pulled from Ford's Mustang, the new shape was more fluid and angular, displaying swept horizontal surfaces that were a radical departure from the curvaceous contours that Michelotti had relied on. The sidelight clusters and bright trim that had graced the flanks of the TR4A were removed for a cleaner profile, while the superfluous power bulge was removed from the broad hood. With the headlights relocated to the outboard extremes of the nose and a Kamm tail, reminiscent of the Aston Martin DB6, the car looked lower and wider, despite retaining the same external dimensions as its predecessor.

The new styling bestowed additional benefits beyond the obvious gains in modernity, providing more luggage capacity in the boot and increased body rigidity made possible by connecting the two rear wings with a vertical panel at the back of the car. Triumph's only contribution to the whole exercise was the replacement of the Surrey removable hardtop with an angular version that was formed into a single unit, better matching the new model's crisper lines.

In keeping with current design trends, Karmann abandoned much of the previous model's brightwork, choosing a matte black grille that bore a horizontal trim strip containing a discrete central badge and eliminating chrome from the flanks. Regardless of the exterior colour, every TR6 had the vertical surface of the Kamm tail painted in flat black, accentuating the modernity of the overall design.

Karmann performed a masterful job with its styling effort for the TR6, creating a thoroughly modern profile while retaining the existing understructure, windscreen frame and the outer panels between the wheel arches.

Although the external dimensions remained the same as before, the TR6 bore a masculine stance that appeared lower and wider than the car that it replaced. This 1972 example features the windscreen surround and sills finished in matte black to provide a more contemporary appearance.

Under the bonnet resided the same 2,498cc six-cylinder engine from the TR5 fitted with the Lucas Mark II petrol injection system. The rated output was 142 bhp (DIN) at 5,700 rpm and 149 pound-feet (DIN) of torque at 3,000 rpm at a 9.5:1 compression ratio.

In the American market, the TR6 retained the same running gear as the TR250 with dual Zenith-Stromberg 175 CD carburettors and an 8.6:1 compression ratio. Output was 104 bhp at 4,500 rpm and 143 pound-feet of torque at 3,000 rpm, allowing acceleration from 0 to 60 mph in 10.7 seconds and a 109 mph top speed.

Simple and economical decals were used to proclaim the identity of the new car, although further embellishment was absent until later in the model run when bolder touches appeared with a Union Jack theme. Rostyle covers were used on the earliest cars, but were replaced with more attractive disc wheels during the first year of production. Wire wheels remained an optional extra. Width for both wire and disc wheels was increased to 5½ inches, requiring the addition of larger fender flares to contain them, with radial tires fitted as standard equipment.

Beneath the new bodywork, the TR6 remained substantially similar to its immediate forebears. An antiroll bar was installed at the front end to reduce the propensity for oversteer in the event that an incautious driver came off the throttle during hard cornering, which also paid additional dividends during more sedate manoeuvres. The IRS suspension, dating back to the TR4A, remained unaltered, though the wider tires provided more grip and improved the ride quality.

Underneath the hood, nothing changed as American customers had to deal with the 104 bhp unit from the TR250, while the rest of the world revelled in the 150 bhp that fuel injection made possible. Inside, revised seats with integrated folding headrests were an option, but standard equipment on US models to meet new safety rules. For more comfort, the Ambla upholstery was dimpled for better ventilation, while adjustable seat backs were introduced during the first year of production.

A very early TR6 featuring Rostyle wheels is shown in this Triumph publicity photograph. (Graham Robson Collection)

To improve cabin ventilation, the rear window in the convertible top could be removed, while the reflective tape on the exterior fabric, which had been introduced on the TR250, continued on the early models sold in North America. The new 15-inch steering wheel and shift knob were trimmed in leather, helping create the most luxurious TR cabin ever. It was also the most informative, featuring warning lights to indicate electrical system discharge, oil pressure loss and braking system malfunction. A dipping rear view mirror made night driving more comfortable and hazard lights were a welcome addition as a warning to traffic when you were stuck on the side of the road.

A Welcome Surprise

The first TR6s were built in September 1968, scarcely more than one year since Karmann received approval for its design proposal. The TR5 had been in production for less than thirteen months, and the TR250 for fourteen, making it rather unlikely that a new model would appear so soon.

Whether it was the unexpected arrival or appreciation for the successful makeover, customers took to the TR6 at once. Especially in the United States, where the decision to forego fuel injection resulted in a very reasonable purchase price, buyers found it an exceptional value, particularly given the nice interior and handsome body. While the motoring press in America clamoured for more power, everyone agreed that the new sheet metal was a very welcome change.

Most writers also appreciated what the TR6 represented: a real commitment from Triumph that it would remain in the game even as former rivals like the Austin-Healey 3000, Morgan Plus 4 and Sunbeam Alpine were leaving the scene. The sports car market, which had evolved through the 1960s, was vastly changed from the days when British sports cars ruled the roost, or at least the less expensive end of it. Sports coupés and saloons were replacing the roadster as the preferred performance layout as embodied by the Datsun 240Z and its successors, who would outsell the TR6 by almost six to one in head-to-head competition.

Despite the changing tide, thousands of buyers still desired traditional sports cars, and Triumph was there to sell them. For those that mourned the Big Healey's recent demise, the TR6 provided succour. *Autocar* summarised its appeal:

> Even if the Austin-Healey 3000 had not been dropped, the TR6 would have taken over as the he-man's sports car in its own right. It is very much a masculine machine, calling for beefy muscles, bold decisions and even ruthlessness on occasions. It could be dubbed the last of the real sports cars, because it displays many of the qualities so beloved in vintage times. In spite of all this (although many would say because), it is a tremendously exhilarating car to drive anywhere.

At least for the earliest examples, assembly quality seemed far better than before, which was odd considering the antiquated body-on-frame construction

The cabin of this 1971 TR6 is a familiar sight to anyone with a passing knowledge of the Michelotti cars, although the wood dashboard acquired a matte finish and the switchgear was modified to enhance safety in an accident. There were a number of seat variations featured throughout the long production run, all provided with head restraints to comply with existing crash standards.

Although the instrument graphics, bezels and operating details changed over time, the basic dash layout remained in use from the TR4 through to the TR6, although the number of warning lights proliferated over time. American anti-theft regulations forced the relocation of the tumbler assembly to under the steering column, which presents an ergonomic challenge familiar to anyone that has operated a TR6 with this feature, especially at night.

Although the Kamm tail was invented in the 1930s, it experienced a renaissance in the 1960s. A number of manufacturers from Aston Martin to Ferrari used this aerodynamic aid for their sporting models. The Lucas rear light assembly was a handsome solution to the lighting requirements of the time. This 1972 Pimento coloured example features the early style number plate lamp.

Although the fixed rear panel made it more difficult to remove the spare tire from the recessed well in the boot, it increased the rigidity of the bodyshell, eliminating some of the rattles that plagued previous models. Note that the rear panel is correctly finished in matte black.

remained unchanged. *Motor Trend* remarked 'we found this particular example freer of rattles than any TR we've driven', while another publication boasted 'there is a feeling of awesome solidity, as though the basic car were carved out of a single block of steel'.

While such positive comments were welcome, Triumph knew that competing against rivals from Germany and Japan on quality was a fool's errand. Instead, the TR6 needed to focus on tradition and fun, where open-air motoring, capable handling and crisp performance were more important than whether the odd part fell off here and there. Most importantly, the TR6 was a bargain, especially when weighed against the European competitors, who were more expensive and less reliable.

From its formal introduction in 1969, sales increased every year until 1974, at annual levels that only the TR3A had surpassed. The outstanding value it represented did not escape notice from the press. *Motor* opined:

> While some other mass production sports cars become gradually tamer and outperformed and outhandled by an ever-faster rash of sporting saloons, the Triumph TR has stood apart from the common herd. In its latest form the TR6 represents what is probably the best value for money in open top terms.

A Dying Breed

Given the TR6's short gestation period, there were remarkably few revisions made to the car during its nine-year production run, validating the inherent goodness of the original package. Of course, given the consistent demand, Triumph had little incentive to devote diminishing resources to refining the product. With affordability such an important virtue, changes were limited to only what was cheap to implement, necessary to comply with new regulations, or done to lower production costs.

73

To illustrate, 1970 models received windscreen frames that were painted in black, regardless of exterior colour, to accord with contemporary design trends, with silver paint replacing the chrome plating on the rocker valve cover and a fan with seven blades replaced one with eight. A more important change was made in mid-1971, when a more robust gearbox with revised ratios was installed to rationalise production with the unit from the contemporary Stag. A simple but effective spoiler was added underneath the front bumper in late 1972 to combat lift at high speeds, along with a plastic grille to replace the fresh air intake flap and wiper arms, painted in matte black. The fan also gained an additional six blades, for an unlucky thirteen in total, but the most significant change to occur was an unfortunate one for enthusiastic drivers.

Introduced in 1973 to address customer complaints over erratic idling and poor running at low speeds in cars equipped with Lucas fuel injection, or so

In order to comply with new 5 mph impact requirements in America, Triumph introduced massive rubber overriders with the 1974 models. Although somewhat inelegant, they are a far sight better than the massive appendages fitted to the MGB and MG Midget. The plastic chin spoiler first appeared in 1973. Note that the increased bumper height on this 1975 model forced the relocation of the running lights and turn signal indicators. (John Goodman)

This 1974 Federal model displays the rubber overriders attached to the rear bumper, where they were positioned over the joints in the multi-piece assembly. The Union Jack decal on the rear wing arrived in the American market for 1973 models and remained in use until the end.

There were several variants of hoods used for the TR6. This example dates from 1971 and shows the correct finish and fasteners. Although most examples were fitted with black hoods, it was possible to special order white as an option.

The squared Kamm tail provided the TR6 with a purposeful look that continues to look modern almost fifty years since it first appeared. The dual exhaust tips in this location are an aftermarket addition.

Triumph alleged, the 'rest of the world' models received a new camshaft with revised timing. This change reduced power from 150 bhp to 125 bhp, although the actual loss was less due to differences in how those figures were calculated. But the effect from behind the wheel was noticeable, making the improved refinement and tractability somewhat bittersweet. At least one automotive historian, Bill Piggott, has argued that the reduction was made to preserve the Stag's reputation, which was considerably slower than the venerable TR6. Because the reduction was not announced publicly, it caught many buyers unaware when they realized that the TR6 was slower than before and they soon filled the corporate inbox with complaints.

The Laycock de Normanville A-type overdrive that had been used since the TR2 was replaced at the same time by an improved J-type unit, which was made standard equipment for rest of the world vehicles the following year, although it operated on the highest two gears, instead of the upper three as before. Along with the camshaft revisions, much of the interior trim was revised and updated. Integrated headrests, which had been used on US examples since 1969, appeared on rest of the world models, while a smaller steering wheel and instruments enhanced with improved graphics and upward pointing needles also arrived on the scene. After years of declining interest, wire wheels were withdrawn as an option, although the disc wheels received silver satin paint on the centre caps as compensation.

Of course, the loss of power that affected worldwide buyers only brought the performance closer to the levels that Americans had been living with since the beginning. At least in the United States, the TR6 was holding its own in the face of increasingly stringent pollution controls and safety requirements that were strangling the life out of its competition.

Unlike the MGB, which was struggling to cope with the standards, and seeing its performance suffer appreciably as a result, Triumph engineers did a

This unique steering wheel was only available for the 1969 model year. The drilled holes were deemed a possible safety hazard, accounting for the appearance of the steering wheel with thin slots that was used in several finishes until the final TR6 rolled off the assembly line in 1976.

This 1971 TR6 shows off the Karmann styling to good effect. The thinner grille opening conveys the appearance of a larger automobile and the smooth surfaces are an important part of the model's continuing appeal.

creditable job of meeting the same challenges. Even with increasingly stringent regulations, Triumph maintained power at around 105 bhp throughout the entire production run even though the compression ratios fell over time. These same engineers also managed to preserve the integrity of the original Karmann design, despite being forced to address issues that had never been considered when the car was new.

In 1974, new American impact requirements mandated installation of bulky rubber overriders, and the following year, the front bumper was raised to just underneath the headlight rims, requiring repositioned turn signal and marker lights. As objectionable as these changes were, they were a far sight better than the grotesque appendages grafted to the front and rear of the MGB and Midget. When compared to its Abingdon-built rivals, the TR6 weathered the safety mandates more tastefully and with a more attractive final solution. Apart from the overriders that can be removed with little effort, there is little to distinguish the very first TR6 from the last one, helping no doubt to account for its evergreen popularity.

Around the same time, however, the worsening labour situation in the United Kingdom was having a deleterious effect on the construction of the cars. The title of an article published by *Motorsport* in November 1973 tells the tale: 'TR6 – 5,000 miles of misery, 5,000 miles of fun.' It reported 'so many faults that it might well have been the first car off the line of a new model. Its general finish was appalling, mechanically it was dreadful and it was to be another 5,500 miles before this Lucas-injected motor car was to run consistently on six cylinders'. Unfortunately, these quality control issues were only a harbinger of worse to come, resulting in disaster for the British automotive industry.

Notwithstanding these serious developments, the TR6 soldiered on, continuing to find buyers for its peculiar blend of traditional and modern qualities. Because so little money was spent on improvements, Triumph's dealers made out like bandits, especially in the United States, where one executive called it a 'fantastic money spinner' that generated profits five times higher than the national average. An increasing array of optional equipment became available over time, including air conditioning, redline tires, a cigarette lighter and an eight-track cassette player, which all helped increase the profit margins to keep dealers happy.

Almost without explanation, production increased in 1973 to 14,825 units, which marked the model's peak, but the following year was almost as good with 12,512 examples sold. Given these solid results, British Leyland, in the midst of another financial crisis, was content to continue with the TR6 as long as it could attract buyers, even as Triumph's engineers and designers were hard at work on the first completely new TR since 1952.

Outside factors, however, were limiting the potential customer pool as the mid-1970s approached. The 1973 oil embargo, imposed by members of the Organization of Arab Petroleum Exporting Countries (OAPEC) in the wake of the Yom Kippur war, restricted petroleum supplies to threatening levels, dampening enthusiasm for sports cars, even those as economical to operate as the TR6.

Much worse was the 1973–74 stock market crash, which saw the value of the Dow Jones Industrial Average benchmark virtually halve in less than two years, while the London Stock Exchange shed almost three quarters of its worth over the same period. This severe economic climate had a deleterious effect on sales, pushing the previously successful TR6 over the proverbial cliff.

British Leyland was in even more desperate straits than usual and would require government assistance to survive. The last rest of the world model departed Canley on 7 February 1975, rendered surplus to requirements by the growing recession. Surprisingly, Triumph continued to manufacture cars for the US until 15 July 1976, with the final few sold throughout the first few months of the following year.

Despite the precarious global financial situation, 6,083 units were built for Americans in 1976, which meant that the TR6 survived long enough to be sold alongside the TR7 for almost eighteen months. Benefitting from the longest TR production run, the TR6 sold better than its predecessors, accounting for 91,850 cars in total.

There would be other British sports cars built in the years to come, including such luminaries as the Aston Martin Vantage, Lotus Esprit, Jaguar F-Type and McLaren F1, but the masculine, hairy-chested persona that the TR6 embodied would never be seen again. Its demise marked the end of an era – even the next TR was something altogether different from the handsome anachronism. It would be missed.

Chapter 6
Triumph TR in Competition

Among the most famous British sports car manufacturers, Triumph's competition record remains one of the least celebrated, but the actual results from works and private efforts tell a story that marque enthusiasts should cherish with pride. The TR in competition often overcame long odds, inconsistent factory support and limited resources to succeed under conditions that would have doomed lesser machinery to failure.

In the first few years after the Second World War, Triumph had little interest in motorsports, which was just as well because it had neither an automobile suitable for the task nor an individual who could lead such an effort. Following his impromptu evaluation of the 20TS following the 1952 London Motor Show at Earls Court, Kenneth Richardson came on board as a developmental engineer for Triumph's nascent sports car project. An experienced racing hand, he had worked for both English Racing Automobiles (ERA) before and British Racing Motors (BRM) after the war, serving primarily as a test driver.

Having delivered such scathing criticism of the hastily constructed prototype, Richardson was tasked with making it better. In a matter of months, Richardson and a small team had remedied the demonic handling and extracted enough power from the Vanguard-based engine to create a proper sports car. With the TR2's record-breaking performance on the highway at Jabbeke, all that remained was to prove itself in actual competition.

Off to the Races

Despite the success in Belgium, Triumph remained uncertain about how to proceed in motorsports, forcing privateers to lead the model into battle. The TR2's maiden outing took place at the 1954 RAC International rally, where Johnny Wallwork secured an unlikely overall victory against works teams from Ford and Rootes. Almost as impressive, TR2 owners also finished in second and fifth, while a female driver took home the Ladies Award.

Not long afterwards, *Autosport* editor Gregor Grant and Peter Reece drove a factory-owned car in the Rallye Lyon-Charbonnières, where they finished third in class, notwithstanding that their stock example had been loaned out from the press pool. A few weeks later, Grant finished seventeenth overall at the Dutch Tulip Rally in the same vehicle, showing the new model's vast potential, despite an amateur at the wheel and a standard engine under the bonnet.

By this time, many in the industry were wondering what the factory was up to, but Richardson and his team were hard at work preparing cars for the Mille Miglia and Alpine Rally at their Banner Lane workshop. Rather than a fully committed effort, however, the single vehicle entrant for the iconic Italian race

Officially a private entry, Edgar Wadsworth and Bob Dickson benefitted from the lessons learned at the Mille Miglia to finish fifteenth overall at the 24 Hours of Le Mans in 1954. Their TR2 maintained a 75 mph average despite a slipping clutch and heavy rain, completing eighty-eight fewer laps than the winning Ferrari 375. (Graham Robson)

At the 1954 Alpine Rally, Maurice Gatsonides (behind the wheel) and Rob Slotemaker finished an impressive sixth overall and received a Coupe des Alpes for an unpenalised run. Triumph also took home the coveted Team Prize, setting the stage for an unprecedented run of success on the rally circuit. (Graham Robson)

Ninian Sanderson and Bob Dickson shared PKV 376 at the 1955 24 Hours of Le Mans. Each of the three works entries ran with some form of disc brakes. This example was the only one to feature disc brakes at all four corners, using an experimental system from Dunlop. Pictured just behind is Lance Macklin's Austin-Healey 100S, which would soon be involved in a collision with Pierre Levegh's Mercedes-Benz 300 SLR. The accident became the worst tragedy in motorsports history, resulting in the death of more than eighty spectators. (Austin-Healey Club of America)

Triumph took the first five places in class at the 1956 Alpine rally with Coupes des Alpes for each. The magnificent showing provided Triumph with the first Coupe des Alpes des Constructeurs ever awarded. From left, the factory drivers were Tommy and Ann Wisdom, Paddy Hopkirk and Willy Cave, and Maurice Gatsonides and Ed Pennybacker. (Graham Robson)

was merely an endurance test to help prepare a fully supported effort for the French Alpine later in the summer.

In a pattern that would recur throughout the rest of Richardson's tenure, the TR2, registered OVC 276, that entered in the Mille Miglia remained in standard tune, but was fitted with an uprated overdrive unit, aero screens, special dampers and 16-inch wire wheels. Behind the wheel was Dutchman Maurice Gatsonides, a former Monte Carlo rally champion, while Richardson served as navigator. With 378 teams present at the start, the race was hotly contested, especially since the minimally prepped Triumph was in the same class as several Italian thoroughbreds, like the Alfa Romeo 1900, Ferrari 500 Mondial, Lancia Aurelia, Maserati A6GCS and OSCA MT4. All things considered, the TR2 performed admirably, avoiding any mechanical failures on the way to a seventh in class finish and twenty-seventh place overall.

Only two months later, Triumph entered a trio of works cars for the French Alpine Rally, driven by a team that was thrown together during the weeks leading up to the event. With a course that ran over the highest passes in the Alps, this was a gruelling event for both car and driver, but Gatsonides and his navigator Rob Slotemaker were up to the task, completing their run sans penalties for a Coupe des Alpes and a second in class finish. Better yet, in its first official outing, Triumph secured the prestigious Team Prize.

Under Richardson's guidance the factory team began to appear more often, but privately owned examples continued to shine at major and minor events around the globe. Just before the Alpine Rally, an entrant driven by Edgar Wadsworth and John Brown crossed the finish line at the 24 Hours of Le Mans in fifteenth place, although the car was not classified for failing to cover 70 per cent of the class winner's distance. At the Tourist Trophy race in Ireland, Triumph secured both the first and second team prizes as all six cars entered ran strong through the finish. The TR2 was no less successful across the Atlantic, where it won the Sports Car Club of America (SCCA) E Production National Championship with Bob Salzgaber at the wheel, while other drivers secured several victories with the new model throughout the long season.

A Formal Affair

The success achieved with the TR2 throughout 1954 led to the formation of a formal competitions programme at Banner Lane. Unlike many companies that had a set roster of drivers, Triumph settled on an assortment of talent that changed with unsettling regularity. Even more curious was Richardson's refusal to specially tune the engines or improve the stock transmission, brakes and suspensions, arguing that such measures were unnecessary to win. At least the vehicles, sourced straight from the assembly line, were carefully assembled, as each individual component was removed and carefully scrutinised before replacement on the cars.

Even for road racing, where speed and handling were as important as outright reliability, Richardson refused to alter his position, although steps were taken to

The works entries for the 1957 Tulip Rally. Pictured are John Waddington, Tom Gold, June Gold, Willy Cave and Ken Richardson on the far right. Missing are Paddy Hopkirk and John Garvey who drove TRW 737. Waddington would pilot TRW 736 to a first in class finish in Holland with Hopkirk close behind in third. The same three cars then competed at Liège-Rome-Liège, where they received the Team Prize. (Graham Robson)

Paddy Hopkirk MBE at the 1958 Alpine Rally in the run that ended his career as a works driver for Triumph. Suffering a punctured tire on his way up the Stelvio Pass, Hopkirk pushed on and cooked his engine in the process, which infuriated Richardson so much that he sacked him after the race. Paddy would bounce back and won the 1964 Monte Carlo Rally in a Mini Cooper S. (Graham Robson)

reduce weight, improve aerodynamics and increase lighting for endurance races. For the 1955 24 Hours of Le Mans, the three works entries were fitted with a pair of experimental disc braking systems to test their suitability for production. One car had Dunlop disc brakes at all four corners, while the remaining pair utilised Girling front disc brakes with 11-inch drums at the back. In a race that is remembered for the horrible accident between Pierre Levegh's Mercedes-Benz 300 SLR and Lance Macklin's Austin-Healey 100S that killed more than eighty spectators, Triumph's team finished the race in respectable fashion, placing fourteenth, fifteenth, and nineteenth overall.

Like Austin-Healey and MG, Triumph accepted that the performance gap between their vehicles and the front-runners at Le Mans was too great to close, forcing all three into a temporary hiatus from the famous race. With the advent of the TR3 and its front disc brakes, rugged construction and prodigious torque, success on the world's rally circuits continued at events such as the Dutch Tulip, French Alpine, Liège-Rome-Liège, Lyon-Charbonnières, Monte Carlo, RAC and Tourist Trophy. In 1956, Triumph again took team honours at the Alpine rally and an impressive five Coupes des Alpes, while a TR3 completed the difficult run from Liège-Rome-Liège at fifth overall.

While Triumph was absent at Le Mans, it sent a three-car team to Florida for the 1957 Sebring 12-Hour Grand Prix of Endurance and won first and second in class at the prestigious endurance event. As the end of the decade approached, Triumph began to fall behind the Big Healeys on the rally circuit, which produced far more power from their highly tuned powerplants and were driven by some of the best drivers in the business.

Triumph returned to the Circuit de la Sarthe in 1959, supported in the endeavour by Alick Dick and Harry Webster, eager for the publicity that a good showing would provide. Richardson constructed a trio of specially prepared examples, featuring fiberglass bodies, lengthened frames, stiffer suspensions, and power from the experimental twin-cam 1,985cc Sabrina engine. Surprisingly, despite all the effort, the racers were heavier than their production counterparts and the new bodywork conferred little aerodynamic advantage. Dubbed the TR3S, all three cars failed to finish, two due to cooling fans that shed their blades and one to an oil cooler failure after twenty-two hours, although the potential from the new powerplant was evident.

For the 1960 24 Hours of Le Mans, Triumph produced four new entrants known as the TRS, built upon the rolling chassis and running gear from the previous year's TR3S, but with fiberglass bodywork styled to approximate Michelotti's Zoom prototype to test the public response to the new shape. Incredibly, the new cars were even heavier than before, tipping the scales at 2,180 pounds, while their top speed barely increased at 128.6 mph. In the race, all three cars suffered from valve damage, reducing their power, although all managed to finish, with the best result at fifteenth overall.

With Triumph in the throes of another financial crisis, the budget for the competition programme was slashed to the bone, allowing the team to enter

Triumph constructed three TR3S racecars for the 1959 24 Hours of Le Mans. Although resembling the standard TR3A, they featured a frame with a wheelbase that was 6 inches longer, fiberglass body panels and were powered by the dual overhead camshaft Sabrina engine. Driven in the race by Peter Bolton and Mike Rothschild, XHP 940 retired after a broken fan blade punctured the radiator in the fourth hour. (Graham Robson)

XHP 939 and XHP 940 at the 1959 24 Hours of Le Mans. Ninian Sanderson and Claude Dubois shared driving duties for XHP 939, which retired after 114 laps after a broken fan blade holed the radiator. (Graham Robson)

The Sabrina dual overhead camshaft engine seen in a TRS. Clearly visible are the twin-choke SU carburettors and the front covers that led to the memorable Sabrina moniker. In racing tune it was capable of producing 150 to 160 bhp. (Graham Robson)

The four TRS racers were built on the rolling chassis of the 1959 TR3S Le Mans entries, retaining the same running gear and four-wheel disc brakes, but utilising fiberglass bodywork based on the Zoom prototypes. This photograph was taken outside the Allesley Service Department. (Graham Robson)

As Ken Richardson looks on at the edge of the open door, Mike Rothschild climbs aboard 928 HP at the 1960 24 Hours of Le Mans. Despite suffering from valve problems that afflicted all three works entries, Rothschild and Les Leston finished eighteenth overall, although their 252 laps were insufficient to earn official classification. (Graham Robson)

The TRS had a much better showing at the 1961 edition of the 24 Hour race at Le Mans. Keith Ballisat and Peter Bolton drove 926 HP to ninth overall, while Les Leston and Rob Slotemaker finished just two spots behind. The showing was good enough to earn Triumph the Manufacturers' Team Prize, which had been in Alick Dick's sights from the start of the Sabrina era. (British Sports Car Hall of Fame)

only the Tulip and Acropolis rallies and Le Mans with the TRS. A lone Herald competed in the Netherlands, while a TR3A finished second in class behind an Austin-Healey 3000 in Greece. In a rarity for his tenure, Richardson's assault on the 24 Hours of Le Mans was provided with sufficient financial support and the money was used to specially tune the engines for more power and improve the suspensions with wider tracks and rack and pinion steering.

Although their weight remained the same and nothing could improve their bluff bodywork, the cars performed spectacularly, turning in faster lap times with bulletproof reliability. The best of the trio finished ninth overall and the others came in eleventh and fifteenth, allowing Triumph to take home the Team Prize for the first time.

Under New Ownership
Not long afterwards, however, worsening financial troubles forced Triumph into Leyland's waiting arms, forcing closure of the competitions department in brutal fashion. Within weeks after the takeover, the racecars were stripped down for inspection and the team members scattered to the wind. Despite the unfortunate development, Harry Webster persisted with demands that the programme resume, allowing him to install a recently hired engineer and experienced rally navigator named Graham Robson to assume the role of Competitions Secretary.

Triumph authorised Italian tuning specialist Conrero to build four cars for use at the 1961 24 Hours of Le Mans. The Leyland merger put those plans to rest after construction of a single example and that car never turned a wheel in anger. Powered by the Sabrina engine, but fitted with a far more aerodynamic body than the TRS, it could have acquitted itself well in the legendary endurance race. It is currently undergoing restoration in the United Kingdom. (Graham Robson)

5VC was one of the four works rally cars prepared under Graham Robson's watch after he became Triumph's Competitions Secretary in February 1962. In this photograph it is shown undergoing preparation for the 1963 Monte Carlo Rally, where it was driven by Jean-Jacques Thuner and finished second in class. A true workhorse, this car competed in numerous rallies, including the Dutch Tulip, French Alpine, Liège-Sofia-Liège, Geneva, RAC, Monte Carlo, RAC and Shell 4000. It found the podium three times and twice was a GT Team Prize winner. For his rally successes and long career as an automotive historian, Robson would earn induction into the British Sports Car Hall of Fame. (Graham Robson)

As was so often the case with Triumph, the resurrected competitions department lacked much in the way of budget, resources or personnel, but at least it had four TR4s to work with. With such little money available, the team operated on a shoestring, doing their best to make the frames stronger, while also reducing weight. Robson was also determined to extract more power from the 2,138cc engine, aware that privateers and specialists were able to make far more horsepower than the factory ever had. Unlike the case during the Richardson era, these racers would feature highly tuned engines, fitted with Weber carburettors, hotter camshaft profiles, tubular exhaust manifolds and modified cylinder heads, allowing them to make almost 130 bhp.

While the TR4 was able to secure an occasional class victory, such as in the 1962 Alpine Rally, there was no avoiding the fact that the competition, primarily in the form of the Big Healeys, had grown too formidable and the nature of rallying and the various classification rules were proving an insurmountable hurdle to overcome.

In the United States, however, it was a different story, as privateers were campaigning both the TR3A and TR4 with great success. Among the most successful was R. W. 'Kas' Kastner, who worked for Cal Sales, which operated the Triumph franchise in Los Angeles, California. With an employer that saw the marketing value in a successful racing programme, Kastner had already won several championships in his TR2 and TR3. With 'never be beaten by equipment' as his personal motto, Kastner was a tuning genius, using carefully ported and polished cylinder heads, modified valves, higher compression ratios, flowed manifolds, special exhaust headers, and revised camshaft profiles to obtain 150 bhp from the 2,138cc engine.

Cal Sales ceased operation as an independent entity in 1960, taken over by the factory in a move to gain better control over its distribution network. As the resident expert, Kastner, with support from Michael Cook, Standard-Triumph USA's advertising and public relations director in New York, developed a plan to campaign a trio of factory-backed cars at the 1963 Sebring 12-Hour Grand Prix of Endurance. While Kastner had great experience racing with the SCCA, the Florida event was held under FIA rules, requiring far more paperwork than he was used to.

R. W. 'Kas' Kastner standing behind the three factory entrants at the 1963 Sebring 12-Hour Grand Prix of Endurance. In his maiden effort at a World Sportscar Championship event, Kastner prepared the trio magnificently, allowing them to finish first, second and fourth in class. Although there was no Team Prize officially awarded that year, Triumph would have earned the laurels. (Kas Kastner)

R. W. 'Kas' Kastner stands before his racing progeny at the 2010 Kastner Cup race at the Mazda Raceway Laguna Seca. In the foreground is the TR250K, which he designed with Pete Brock. An early retirement at the 1968 Sebring 12-Hour Grand Prix of Endurance, it is currently campaigned on the vintage racing circuit in the United States. Kastner would be included in the inaugural class of the British Sports Car Hall of Fame in 2017. (Cape Coventry Racing)

With homologation documents flown over from London at the last minute, Kastner assembled a crack team that included Americans Bob Tullius, Charlie Gates, Bob Cole, Bruce Kellner and Ed Diehl, while Peter Bolton and Mike Rothschild came from England. Facing a grid that contained some of the best drivers in the world, such as Phil Hill, Richie Ginther, Ken Miles, John Fitch, Pedro Rodriguez and John Surtees, the three TR4s finished first, second and fourth in class, the only complete team to reach the finish line.

With that impressive showing as proof of his ability, Kastner was named the Competition Manager for Triumph in the United States. For the Canadian Shell 4000 rally in 1964, Kastner prepared three TR4s that had formerly served as Robson's factory rally mounts, but fitted with new chassis frames and converted to left-hand drive. In a far cry from the decade earlier, the cars were fitted with aluminium outer panels, Weber carburettors, limited-slip differentials, and Perspex for the backlights and side windows. Although their overall placement was a disappointment, Triumph took home the Team Prize, which helped gain valuable publicity for the marque in North America.

For much of the rest of the decade, Triumph focused on the Spitfire for endurance events in Europe, but the TR4 and TR4A continued their successful run in the United States. In 1966, Kastner repeated his earlier feat at the Sebring 12-Hour Grand Prix of Endurance, where the entire team swept its class in a race marred by the death of Bob McLean, who was trapped in his burning GT40 after a terrible shunt.

The Winning Standard

Notwithstanding Kastner's success at Sebring and his support of several SCCA national championship winners in his capacity as the North American racing supremo, Bob Tullius holds the undisputed crown as Triumph's most successful driver and team operator. Back in 1961, Tullius was selling office equipment for Eastman Kodak, but raced his TR3A almost every weekend with the SCCA. With a spate of successful outings under his belt, Tullius started to telephone Triumph's North American headquarters on an almost daily basis, seeking a new TR4. After creating a nuisance with his campaign, Tullius held a meeting with the company's executives in New York, but Triumph's financial situation was precarious in the midst of the Leyland takeover and it could not grant his request.

The following year his victory streak continued, even against the TR4 that had just started to appear in force. Eventually, Martin Tustin, the company's chief executive in the United States, relented and shipped a new model to the bold young driver. Although that example was promptly wrecked, he rebuilt it using parts from several parts cars, and then resumed winning races. Beyond his obvious talent behind the wheel, Tullius was a master promoter, who could charm sponsors and then deliver the publicity that they sought in return.

With an SCCA national championship already on his resume, Tullius also captured the chequered flag at the inaugural American Road Race of Champions. By this time, his team, called Group 44 Racing, had become the gold standard in sports car racing, famed for their maniacal attention to detail and professional demeanour. In 1965, Tullius secured a sponsorship agreement with Quaker State, an American oil company, which allowed him to expand his burgeoning racing empire.

Operating from a base in Fairfax, Virginia, Bob Tullius started to win races immediately after receiving his competition license. He started his career in a TR3A, before moving on to a steady succession of Triumph machinery. Later he created and campaigned the legendary Jaguar XJR. (Steve Knoll)

Group 44 Racing Inc. would prove one of the most successful teams in American motorsports. The immaculate green and white racers, christened 'The White Wave', would win fourteen SCCA national championships, three Trans-Am championships and eleven IMSA victories, while Tullius would be inducted into the International Motorsports Hall of Fame, SCCA Hall of Fame and British Sports Car Hall of Fame. (Steve Knoll)

Tullius and his court of drivers would go on to win countless races, including several national championships, in all manner of Triumphs from the various TRs to the smaller Spitfires and GT6s. In the process, he changed the face of motorsports with his comprehensive sponsorship packages and the successful promotional blitz that inevitably followed his victories. Even the TR250 and TR6, which had to race against exceptional machinery from Datsun and Porsche, proved almost unbeatable when racing in his familiar white and green livery.

While Group 44 Racing certainly authored the most numerous competition successes through the 1960s and 1970s, Triumphs continued to compete around the world. Kastner campaigned the landmark TR250K, designed with Pete Brock, at the 1968 Sebring 12-Hour Grand Prix of Endurance, but the car retired in the first few hours after a rear wheel failed on the track. Although it should have served as the basis for future factory efforts, the TR250K retired after its maiden outing, hastening Kastner's departure in 1970. He continued to campaign Triumphs in an official capacity through his own Kastner-Brophy team, finding occasional success and showing the colours in his own inimitable fashion.

While the TR7 and TR8 would continue to rally and race with success over the coming years, the wedges never fully supplanted their predecessors in the hearts and minds of Triumph enthusiasts. Even in the twenty-first century, Triumphs continue to compete and win on the vintage racing circuit, even capturing another SCCA National Championship in 2009 with Sam Halkias behind the wheel. Not a bad result for a car that ended production almost thirty-five years earlier, showing that where there are Triumphs, victories will surely follow.

Bibliography

Allen, Dave and Dick Strome. *Triumph Guide*. (New York: Sports Car Press, 1959)

Carver, Mike, and Nick Seale and Anne Youngson. *British Leyland Motor Corporation: 1968–2005 The Story from Inside*. (Stroud: The History Press, 2015)

Church, Roy. 'Deconstructing Nuffield: The evolution of managerial culture in the British motor industry.' *Economic History Review 49* (1996).

Cook, Michael. 'Triumph Takes a Holiday.' *Automobile Quarterly* 32 (1993) 22–35.

Cook, Michael. *Triumph Cars in America*. (St Paul: Motorbooks International, 2001)

Grant, Gregor. *British Sports Cars*. (Los Angeles: Floyd Clymer, 1948)

Harvey, Chris. *TR for Triumph*. (Somerset: The Oxford Illustrated Press, 1983)

Harvey, Chris. 'Triumph Before Tragedy.' *Automobile Quarterly* 28 (1990) 10–29.

Hodges, David. *Essential Triumph TR: TR2–TR8*. (Devon: Bay View Books, 1994)

Kastner, Kas. *Kas Kastner's Historical & Technical Guide for Triumph Cars*. (Vista: R. W. Kastner, 2008)

Kastner, Kas. *Kas Kastner's Triumphs: Race Cars, Street Cars and Special Cars*. (Vista: R. W. Kastner, 2010)

Kimberley, William. *Triumph TR6*. (Dorset: Veloce Publishing, 1995)

Knowles, David. *Triumph TR7: The Untold Story*. (Ramsbury: Crowood, 2007)

Knowles, David. *Triumph TR6: The Complete Story*. (Wiltshire: Crowood, 2016)

Krause, G. William. *Triumph Sports Cars*. (St Paul: Motorbooks International, 1998)

Krause, G. William. *Triumph Sports and Racing Cars*. (Forest Lake: Car Tech, 2017)

Langworth, Richard, 'Trundling Along With Triumph.' *Automobile Quarterly* 11 (1973) 116–145.

Newton, Richard. *Illustrated Triumph Buyer's Guide*. (Osceola: Motorbooks International, 1994)

Nikas, John. *Rule Britannia: When British Sports Cars Saved a Nation*. (Philadelphia: Coachbuilt Press, 2017)

Nye, Doug. *British Cars of the Sixties*. (Stillwater: Parker House, 2008)

Piggott, Bill. *Triumph by Name, Triumph by Nature: The Sidescreen TR Compendium*. (Belton: Dalton Watson Fine Books, 1995)

Piggott, Bill. *Triumph: The Sporting Cars*. (Gloucestershire: Sutton Publishing, 2000)

Piggott, Bill. *Triumph TR: TR2 to 6 The last of the traditional sports cars*. (Somerset: Haynes, 2003)

Piggott, Bill. *Triumph: Sport and Elegance*. (Somerset: Haynes Publishing, 2006)

Piggott, Bill. *Triumph TR2, TR3, TR4, TR5, TR6, TR7, TR 8: Collector's Originality Guide*. (Minneapolis: Motorbooks, 2009)

Pressnell, Jon. *Classic British Sports Cars*. (Somerset: Haynes, 2006)

Robson, Graham. *The Story of Triumph Sports Cars*. (Surrey: Motor Racing Publications, 1974)

Robson, Graham. *The Triumph TRs: A Collector's Guide*. (London: Motor Racing Publications, 1981)

Robson, Graham. *Triumph TRs: The Complete Story.* (Ramsbury: Crowood, 1991)

Robson, Graham. *The Works Triumphs: 50 Years in Motorsport.* (Somerset: Foulis, 1993)

Robson, Graham and Richard Langworth. *Triumph Cars: The Complete Story.* (Croydon: MRP Publishing, 2004)

Robson, Graham. *Works Triumphs in Detail.* (Devon: Herridge & Sons, 2014)

Rosenbusch, Karla A. 'Dorothy Deen: The Lady Triumphs.' *Automobile Quarterly* 34 (1995) 48–61.

Stein, Jonathan A. *British Sports Cars in America 1946–1981.* (Kutztown: Automobile Quarterly Publications 1993)

Taylor, James. *Triumph TR.* (Osceola: Motorbooks International, 1997)

Taylor, James. *British Sports Cars of the 1950s and 60s.* (Oxford: Shire Library, 2014)

Whisler, Timothy, 'Niche Products in the British Motor Industry: A History of MG and Triumph Sports Cars.' *Business and Economic History* 22 (1993) 19–24.

About the Author

John Nikas is the author of *Rule Britannia: When British Sports Cars Saved a Nation*, which was the runner-up for the 2017 Mercedes-Benz Award for the Montagu of Beaulieu Trophy. He has published several books on automotive history and frequently speaks at museums, events, and club gatherings. A regular motoring columnist in the United Kingdom, he is a member of the Guild of Automotive Writers, Society of Automotive Historians and the Friends of Triumph. Among his upcoming book projects are *Healey Revealed: The Men and Machines, 44: Bob Tullius and the Birth of Modern Racing* and *Into the Gathering Storm: Classic Motorcars on the Brink of War.*

About the Photographer

Marc Vorgers (1967) studied industrial design and graduated on innovative transportation solutions in Arnhem, the Netherlands, before starting his own design studio in 1992. The founder, in 2000, of the Classicar Garage (www. ClassicarGarage.nl), which is one of the automotive world's most visited websites, Marc has profiled thousands of vintage and classic cars. He has also contributed photographs, historical information and editorials to publications across the continent and the rest of the world.